Quiet Achievers

GLOBAL
PUBLISHING
G R O U P

Global Publishing Group

Australia • New Zealand • Singapore • America • London

Quiet
Achievers

How to be seen and heard so you stand out

MELISSA HAGGARTY

First Edition 2025

Copyright © 2025 Melissa Haggarty

National Library of Australia
Cataloguing-in-Publication entry:

Quiet Achievers: How to be seen and heard so you stand out - Melissa Haggarty

1st ed.
ISBN: 978-1-925370-90-4 (pbk.)
ISBN 978-1-925370-94-2 (ebook)

A catalogue record for this book is available from the National Library of Australia

Published by Global Publishing Group
PO Box 258, Banyo, QLD 4014 Australia
Email admin@globalpublishinggroup.com.au

For further information about orders:
Phone: +61 7 3267 0747

DEDICATION

I dedicate this book to Lily, my beautiful Burmese cat who brought love and joy to my life for over seventeen years. Lily taught me the true meaning of quality of life over quantity. She told me when she was ready to go; she didn't want to wait until she had nothing left in the tank. She taught me about love, grace, playfulness and connection. She was the epitome of authenticity - gentle, loving and most of all, wonderfully sassy. I love you, my beautiful girl.

I also dedicate this book to my Dad. He loved me with all his heart and was always proud of me. Growing up, he would praise my achievements, often followed with, "But you could have done this…..". I took the 'but' to mean I was never good enough. Since his passing he has let me know that he intended the 'but' to push me further and help me achieve more - a beautiful gift from my Dad. He epitomised the Quiet Achiever, working diligently without seeking attention or recognition. He was hard-working, entrepreneurial, had a dry wit and most of all, loved sharing big feasts with his family. I love you, Dad.

Melissa Haggarty

ACKNOWLEDGEMENTS

I want to thank all the people who are in my life and those who have come and gone. You have all taught me valuable lessons and this has shaped the person I am today. I appreciate you.

I wish to acknowledge other Quiet Achievers who have struggled to be seen and heard, and celebrate your significant contributions to the world. Thank you to the leaders and work colleagues who recognise the value and contribution of a Quiet Achiever.

My family, for their love and support. I love knowing that I can call on my family and they will always be there for me. I love you all very much and treasure the time we spend together.

Warren Dowling, you have been one of my greatest supporters. You have enabled me to achieve many things, even when my eyes were as big as saucers. You taught me to prioritise my self-care before work and helped me bring spontaneity into my life.

Sharon Jurd, you changed my life. You have been instrumental in fast-tracking my success. I have learned so much from you. Once you enter into Sharon's world you never want to leave. It's a good place to be. You even pushed me to finish writing this book by saying you were sick of hearing me talk about it and to just get it done.

Alissa Meechan introduced me to the idea of writing a book that resulted in me becoming an International Best Seller Author through a compilation book called Voices of Impact Volume 2. Alissa also introduced me to Sharon Jurd. Alissa is the one I ask to check in with my higher self when I want a secondary check to confirm I'm on the right track.

Andrew Carter, from Global Publishing Group, for believing in my concept for this book and saying yes to publishing *Quiet Achievers – How to be seen and heard so you stand out*. Thank you for the kick up the bum when needed and for the culinary orgasms.

Jacine Greenwood, for helping me nail who I was writing the book for: the Quiet Achievers.

Dr Jannie Grové, you have a brilliant mind, a knack for articulating complex ideas simply and are a true gentleman. You regularly remind me of my brilliance by calling me "Melstar" and frequently sing my praises to others. We are like peas from the same pod in terms of being Quiet Achievers. Your preference for Diet Dr Pepper over a Margarita is questionable; we can work on that.

Nigel Clements, you always remind me to think solutions-focused. I am in awe of how easy the solution is after I discuss challenges with you. You always encourage me to do what makes me happy. I value your consistency, respect and support, and appreciate being able to be 'real' with you. I have shared some of the most memorable laughs in my life with you.

EXTRA BONUSES

FOR YOU!

FREE INSIGHT CALL

I would love to offer you an opportunity to spend 45 minutes with me one-on-one. Let's connect virtually for 45 minutes to discuss anything about you and your work and the changes you desire. I guarantee after our conversation, you will have clarity on what your next step will be. Book your free insight call at
https://integratedsoul.com.au/services/Insight-call/

YOUR PREFERRED REPRESENTATIONAL SYSTEM

Do you want to know your preferred representational system? Is it Visual, Auditory, Kinaesthetic or Auditory Digital? Complete an easy test to find out at
https://integratedsoul.com.au/books/quiet-achievers/

FOR LEADERS

Are you a leader wanting to know how you can empower a Quiet Achiever and help them stand out? Download my top tips with strategies for leaders to help Quiet Achievers shine at
https://integratedsoul.com.au/books/quiet-achievers/

www.integratedsoul.com.au
connect@integratedsoul.com.au

CONTENTS

FOREWORD

I was always told to, "Put your head down and bum up and work hard", and when you do you will get the recognition, pay rise or promotion that you are after. This may have worked for some, but it did not work for me.

As a massive introvert, I was rarely noticed or my achievements taken seriously. I did not want to 'brag' or 'big note' myself to get noticed, but wondered what I needed to do to move forward in my career and business.

I looked around for answers and found nothing. I felt alone with no way of knowing how to change things.

So, I did what I thought I needed to do: work even harder. That was not the answer.

I now speak on large stages and coach people all around the world, own nine companies and am also an international #1 best-selling author. Throughout my journey I found very few people who wanted to talk to me about how to get noticed if you were not the loudest, most extrovert person in the room - which I am definitely not!

What I want you to know is that you are not alone when you feel you are not heard, when you feel you have been passed over for an opportunity, when doors aren't opening for you easily. I have been there and so have others just like you and me.

You may have tried copying other confident, extrovert people hoping for the same results. You may have had your fair share of mistakes and setbacks. I bet you may have even asked yourself, "Why them and not me?" I know I have previously asked this question many times.

Right now, you do not have to go through any more pain, torment, desperation and frustration that you have felt in the past.

What I suggest is to seek out help. Find a coach, the person that just gets you, who can be your biggest advocate as you make changes, do things differently and gain forward momentum. The biggest mistake people make is trying to do it all by themselves. It is so much easier when you have that person to pat you on the back, reassure you and show you how to keep going when you don't want to.

Melissa Haggarty is that person.

For whatever reason you picked up this book or opened the pages, it was meant to be. You have found this book at the right time for you.

You are about to receive the answers you need.

Fortunately, Melissa has decided to write this book for people exactly like you and me.

Melissa has had her own experiences and now wants to share real life strategies to make a difference. She has been there! She knows exactly how you feel. She sees you. She hears you.

Melissa is bringing to light the amazing people contributing to industries, communities, organisations, and the world who are what she calls the 'Quiet Achievers'.

By reading this book you will have all the tools to make considerable change to your life.

If you follow Melissa's steps and tools you will notice how easy it is to achieve your goals and dreams without feeling 'icky', without feeling like a fake, without feeling like you have to be someone else.

You can be the quietest person in the room and be successful. I figured it out the hard way, the long way with plenty of mistakes. In your hand you have the best opportunity to bring to reality your life as it should be with ease and calm. Take notice of Melissa, learn from her, model from her and follow the processes that worked for her.

So, turn to the next page and start celebrating you.

Sharon Jurd
International Speaker, Coach & Author
Director
SMJ Coaching Institute
HydroKleen Global Pty Ltd
HydroKleen Australia Pty Ltd
HydroKleen International Pty Ltd
Jurds Pty Ltd
SMJ (Singleton) Pty Ltd
International best-selling author of 'How to Grow Your Business Faster than Your Competitor' & 'Extraordinary Women in Franchising'.

INTRODUCTION

I was assigned the project of achieving ISO 9001 certification for the processing facility where I worked as the Laboratory Superintendent. ISO 9001 is a quality system that outlines various processes requiring compliance for certification.

I had the support of two amazing women who helped me achieve ISO 9001 certification for the site. I pushed them into the spotlight for their growth as they were Quiet Achievers and because I preferred to stay in the background. As a result, the organisation did not see my contributions and the two women received recognition for their efforts.

When ISO 9001 certification was achieved, management sent an email congratulating them on their work. I found out about this email when a peer, who had previously been my leader in another organisation and was familiar with my work style, forwarded it to me, copied the original email recipients and congratulated me on the project's success.

To this day, my name is not mentioned in this organisation as being responsible for achieving ISO 9001 certification for the site. Anyone who has achieved ISO 9001 for a site will know it is a bucketload of work!

Do you feel invisible at work even though you consistently deliver on time and to a high quality?

Do you feel anxious in meetings when you want to voice your opinion?

Do your work colleagues get noticed because they boast loudly while you work quietly?

After twenty years in my industry career, I felt disconnected, burnt out and uninspired. I no longer felt like I belonged. Despite achieving success, proven by me professionally setting up, commissioning and operating multiple new laboratories, I found myself in an environment that didn't resonate with me.

The culture of the organisation favoured and celebrated Loud Achievers - individuals who were more vocal about their accomplishments and who dominated conversations; people who seemed oblivious to the importance of authentic connections and focused solely on furthering their careers. In this environment it seemed that loudness equated to recognition, overshadowing authentic relationships and genuine engagement.

Working with such individuals felt frustrating; promises made seldom translated into action, leaving me feeling like I was constantly hitting a brick wall. It was like they were Teflon-coated. They would commit to taking action but the commitment didn't stick. Each time I followed up, I would receive a gob fest of words that sounded great however the action didn't exist to match the words.

The Loud Achievers focused on interactions with individuals who could promote or propel them in their careers. I wanted them to be quiet for long enough to hear what I had to say without me having to be in their face and speak louder than normal to be heard. I felt like I had to be aggressive to get recognised.

This experience stood in stark contrast to my previous workplaces where sincerity and respect were abundant. In those environments, leaders and colleagues regularly expressed heartfelt appreciation for a job well done and for lending a helping hand. I felt I could be me at work. I often was the only female and I could express myself. My work life had been a source of pride and I knew I excelled in my role. In this organisation, I felt insignificant and lost. What the hell was going on? Why was I struggling to assert myself professionally?

Challenges arise when an organisation becomes overly saturated with a single personality type.

There were people who appreciated my work; they had collaborated closely with me. They witnessed my capabilities, dedication and knew the quality of my work but the appreciation was few and far between.

I believe in having a diverse range of personalities within an organisation as they bring forth varying strengths and skills to achieve the organisation's goals.

In Quiet Achievers, I share my learnings and practical tools so that Quiet Achievers can learn how to secure the recognition they deserve and organisations can benefit from the value they add in the workplace. Being in a workplace where you feel valued, respected and able to express yourself fully makes a profound difference in your overall well-being and sense of fulfilment.

CHAPTER 1

SPOTLIGHTING THE QUIET ACHIEVER

1 SPOTLIGHTING THE QUIET ACHIEVER

In a world that often celebrates the loudest voices, Quiet Achievers can find themselves overlooked or underestimated. Beneath their unassuming exterior lies a wealth of talent, wisdom and capability waiting to be recognised.

Quiet Achievers possess hidden power and potential as those who prefer to lead with subtlety rather than showmanship. From leaders to team members, their contributions often form the foundation of success, quietly but profoundly shaping outcomes and driving progress.

The paradox of being a Quiet Achiever lies in the conflict between achieving significant success while not seeking attention or acclaim, resulting in a lack of recognition of their success. This paradox highlights the challenge of balancing humility with the need for visibility in environments where recognition and acknowledgment often drive career advancement and opportunities.

KEY ASPECTS OF THE PARADOX CONFLICT THAT QUIET ACHIEVERS FACE

1. Modesty Vs Recognition

Quiet Achievers are modest about their achievements. They are seen as team players who prioritise the team's success over their own success which then creates a positive team culture and work environment.

Quiet Achievers do not receive the recognition they deserve for their work as they do not actively share the status of their work and their accomplishments. This lack of visibility leads to being overlooked for promotions, salary bonuses and opportunities that go to those who are more vocal about their achievements.

2. Contribution Vs Visibility

Quiet Achievers typically make significant contributions through consistent effort and dedication. They focus on results producing high-quality outcomes.

Since Quiet Achievers do not draw attention to their contributions, leaders and peers can be oblivious to their efforts. This creates a lack of awareness about their capabilities and the value they bring to the organisation.

3. Performance Vs Recognition

Quiet Achievers maintain a consistent high level of performance. They are reliable and have a good work ethic making them valuable to any team and organisation.

Consistent high performance without sharing your work status or accomplishments can be taken for granted. Leaders can assume that Quiet Achievers will always deliver high performance without needing acknowledgment or rewards, leading to burnout or frustration for the Quiet Achiever.

4. Career Progression Vs Self-Promotion

Career progression requires visibility, networking and self-promotion. Whilst Quiet Achievers are team players, they may find it challenging to be recognised for career progression opportunities because they do not engage in these activities as much as Loud Achievers.

Self-promotion to a Quiet Achiever can feel inauthentic and uncomfortable. This leads to their achievements being unknown and not being rewarded appropriately.

5. Value Vs Perception

The value of a Quiet Achiever's work can be significant. Their dedication, attention to detail, consistency and persistence contribute to the success of goals and teams.

The perception of others may not match this value. If their achievements are not visible, others may underestimate their contributions, creating a mismatch between their actual impact and how they are perceived within the organisation.

Quiet Achievers must navigate this paradox to obtain recognition for their efforts and the value they add while staying true to their natural preference for high-quality work and staying under the radar.

PERSONALITY LABELS

I generally avoid using labels to stereotype personalities and behaviours as this can lead to incorrect generalisations about individuals, given the complexity of personality preferences. However, using labels can help identify specific traits and behaviours that are predominantly found in certain individuals. With this in mind, I will explain what I mean by certain personality labels.

Let's begin by differentiating between introverts and extroverts. Carl Gustav Jung, the father of analytical psychology, developed the concept of introverts and extroverts in the early twentieth century.

INTROVERTS	EXTROVERTS
Recharge by spending time alone	Recharge by being around other people
Prefer smaller, more intimate gatherings	Prefer large, lively gatherings
More reserved and contemplative	More outgoing and talkative
Thrive in calm, quiet environments	Thrive in busy, stimulating environments

Now let's differentiate between introversion, shyness and quiet achievement.

INTROVERSION	SHYNESS	QUIET ACHIEVEMENT
A personality trait where individuals are more focused on internal thoughts and feelings rather than seeking external stimulation	A feeling of discomfort or anxiety in social situations, due to a fear of judgement by others	Accomplish significant things without seeking attention or recognition
Preference for small groups and need time alone to recharge	Driven by anxiety and fear of social judgement	Preference for modesty and intrinsic motivation
May be socially comfortable and prefer less stimulation and may find social events draining	Feel uncomfortable or anxious in social situations and difficulty initiating conversations or speaking in front of groups	Not necessarily shy or introverted, they prefer to work behind the scenes, let their work speak for itself and do not seek the spotlight

Motivated by the need to recharge and process internally	Motivated by a desire to avoid negative social judgement	Motivated by the satisfaction of their work and results rather than external validation

Shyness can affect both introverts and extroverts. Quiet Achievers can be either introverts or extroverts. Their quietness is about how they handle success rather than social interaction preferences.

Now, let's differentiate between Quiet Achievers and Loud Achievers.

QUIET ACHIEVERS	LOUD ACHIEVERS
Prefer subtle or private acknowledgement	Seek public and explicit recognition
Reserved and understated	Outgoing and expressive
Motivated by personal satisfaction and intrinsic rewards	Motivated by external validation and public praise
Downplay their achievements, often highlighting team efforts	Highlight their successes, often focusing on individual contributions

CHARACTERISTICS OF A QUIET ACHIEVER

Remember, a Quiet Achiever can be shy, an introvert or an extrovert. It is difficult to provide an exact percentage of Quiet Achievers who are either introverts or extroverts. Without precise research data, it is reasonable to assume that Quiet Achievers are most likely introverts due to the similarity between their preferences and working styles.

In summary, when I refer to a Quiet Achiever, these are the characteristics they possess:

- They are consistent, persistent and reliable
- They let their work and results speak for itself
- They celebrate their wins quietly
- They are modest and don't seek attention or recognition
- They take the time to find the right solution
- They are dedicated to excellence
- They have a keen eye for detail, ensuring accuracy and thoroughness in their work
- They are focused on their objectives and meet their role requirements
- They prefer working independently and are self-motivated
- They recognise the value of teamwork and work collaboratively when necessary
- They reflect on their experience and learn from their successes and failures
- They communicate effectively and clearly when they feel they have valuable input

A Quiet Achiever is like a lighthouse, guiding with its steady light without drawing attention to itself.

"Lighthouses don't go running all over an island looking for boats to save; they just stand there shining." **Anne Lamott**

THE IMPORTANCE OF BEING SEEN AND HEARD IN TODAY'S WORLD

"If you think you are too small to make a difference, try sleeping with a mosquito."
Dalai Lama

If you are a Quiet Achiever, that's perfectly OK. It's important to first understand why we behave the way we do and recognise our preferences. However, there are times when we seek specific results and outcomes, and to achieve these goals we need to take action. Often this requires stepping outside of our comfort zone.

In today's interconnected and competitive environment, being seen and heard is essential for career success and advancement, effective communication, making an impact and adapting to work cultures.

To achieve personal and professional success:

- Standing out is crucial for professional advancement
- Visibility leads to recognition, promotions and new opportunities
- Building and nurturing valuable connections requires being known and remembered, both online and offline
- Demonstrating your unique value helps control how others perceive you and enhances your influence
- Being heard ensures your ideas and contributions influence decisions and drive change

- Sharing your expertise establishes you as an authority, enhancing your influence in your field
- Visibility ensures you remain connected and relevant in the workplace
- Active participation in meetings and projects foster better collaboration and strengthens team dynamics

Receiving no recognition for your work feels like your efforts are unappreciated, even when recognition is not your primary driver.

The purpose of this book is to acknowledge your brilliance as a Quiet Achiever and to give you practical tools to get the recognition you deserve if you find yourself in an organisation or reporting to a leader who is not skilled in recognising the value and contribution of a Quiet Achiever.

It's not about changing who you are, it's about empowering Quiet Achievers to step into the spotlight on their own terms and make their mark in the world.

"Life isn't about finding yourself. Life is about creating yourself." **George Bernard Shaw**

Throughout these pages you'll find inspiration, validation and a renewed sense of purpose as you embrace your identity as a Quiet Achiever.

So, let's get you stepping out of the shadows and into the spotlight and be seen and heard in a way that honours your authentic self.

Together, let's celebrate YOU - Quiet Achievers who enrich lives and elevate the world.

CHAPTER 2

GET RECOGNISED WITHOUT FEELING LIKE A SHOW OFF

2 GET RECOGNISED WITHOUT FEELING LIKE A SHOW OFF

My Mum says about me, "Growing up, you were never a show off. You would achieve things and make no noise about it. You would only tell us a few days later about your achievement. You were always in the background, no big noise; you were always this way".

This approach works in the workplace when you have people in your environment who recognise your significant contributions and the value you add. It doesn't work when you don't have these people in your environment and there are simple steps you can take to gain the recognition you deserve.

BUILD RAPPORT

To get recognised, people must like you! We get people to like us through building rapport, specifically using the Neuro-Linguistic Programming (NLP) process of rapport. NLP is a psychological approach that explores the connections between neurological processes (neuro), language (linguistic), and behavioural patterns learned through experience (programming).

We build rapport through our communication, which encompasses more than just the words we speak. Communication includes both verbal and non-verbal elements. At any moment, we are conveying much more than just our spoken words. In fact, non-verbal communication often carries more significance than the words themselves.

Communication can be broken down into the following elements:

Words 7%

Tonality 38%

Physiology 55%

The basis of rapport is when people are similar to each other; they tend to like each other. The NLP process of rapport is about creating a feeling as if the participants like each other. Rapport is a process more about responsiveness than genuine 'liking'.

Rapport is established by matching and/or mirroring the three key elements of communication. In NLP this is known as 'pacing and leading'. The following are examples of how the major elements of communication can be easily 'paced':

55% Physiology	38% Tonality	7% Words
• Posture • Gestures • Facial expression • Blinking • Breathing	• Tone (pitch) • Tempo (speed) • Timbre (quality) • Volume (loudness)	• Predicates (sense specific words) • Key words • Common experiences • Content chunks

Crossover mirroring in NLP is a subtle technique used to build rapport by mirroring a person's behaviour, but in a way that is not directly copying their exact movements. Instead of mirroring the same body part or action, you use a different body part to reflect their actions.

For example:

- If someone is tapping their foot, you might mirror this by subtly tapping your hand
- If someone is moving their head while speaking, you could reflect this movement with a similar rhythm using your hand gestures

The purpose of crossover mirroring is to create a connection without being too obvious, which helps establish rapport by making the other person feel understood and comfortable. Since it's less direct than traditional mirroring, it can be more natural and harder for the other person to notice, yet it still fosters a sense of synchronisation and responsiveness in communication.

Everyone has a preferred representational system. Recognising someone's preferred representational system will allow you to communicate in a way that is more similar to how they communicate inside their own mind. The four representational systems are Visual, Auditory, Kinaesthetic and Auditory Digital. Remember that every person has all four representational systems operating to some extent. The key is to notice their preferred representational system.

VISUAL	AUDITORY	KINAESTHETIC	AUDITORY DIGITAL
People who favour the visual system often stand or sit with their heads and bodies erect with their eyes up. They tend to breathe from the top of their lungs. They often sit forward in their chair and are organised, neat, well-groomed and orderly. They are often thin and wiry (though not always) and they memorise by seeing pictures. Noise usually doesn't distract them. They often have trouble remembering verbal instructions because their minds tend to wander. A visual person will be interested in how things (e.g. your product, service or solution) **LOOK**. Appearances are usually very important to them.	People who favour the auditory system may move their eyes side to side. They usually breathe from the middle of their chest, talk to themselves and can be easily distracted by noise. They can repeat things back to you easily, they learn by listening, and usually like music and talking on the phone. They memorise by steps, procedures and sequences. The auditory person likes to be **TOLD** how they're doing, and responds to a certain tone of voice or set of words. They will be interested in what you have to **SAY** about things (e.g. your product, service or solution).	People who favour the kinaesthetic system typically breathe from the bottom of their lungs and you'll see their stomach go in and out when they breathe. They often move and talk verrry slooowly. They like physical rewards and touching. Also, they usually stand closer to people than a person favouring visual typically would. They memorise by doing or walking through something. They will be interested in things (e.g. your product, service or solution) if it **FEELS** right, or if you can give them something they can grasp.	People who favour the Auditory Digital system will spend a fair amount of time talking to themselves. They will want to know if your product or service **MAKES SENSE**. A person favouring auditory digital can and most likely will exhibit characteristics of the other major representational systems as AD is actually a derived representational system.

The below four indicators will help you know when you have established rapport. You might experience one or more of these indicators, keep in mind, only the fourth indicator (Auditory Digital) is a sure sign you have established rapport.

1

Kinaesthetic

Internal Feeling

You may experience a feeling of warmth. Some people describe the feeling as 'butterflies'.

2

Visual

Colour Shift

There may be a change in colour in both people, usually from the neck up. You will feel it in yourself first and then notice it in the other person. Typically, a shift from light to dark.

3

Auditory

Hear Something

They may say something like:

Do I know you?

Have we met before?

I feel like we've known each other for years.

4

Auditory Digital

Leading

Rapport is when both people are responding to each other.

Sure indicator is when they begin to follow you.

Test by shifting positions, pick up a pen etc.

Rapport is pacing and leading.

The only sure indicator of rapport is leading; when you lead, they follow.

There is lots more to learn about rapport but this will get you started. Start observing other people's behaviour and the way they communicate and match and mirror!

ACTIVITY You can learn your own representational system preference here: https://integratedsoul.com.au/books/quiet-achievers/

Knowing your preferred representational system is beneficial for understanding your communication style. For example, my preferred representational system is Visual. Early in my career, when an Operator would come into the lab and request an analysis, after they left I often had to stop and think which analysis they had requested. Once I learned that my preferred representational system was Visual, I realised that simply hearing the request (Auditory) wouldn't stick with me easily, so to suit my Visual preference, I began carrying a notebook to write down any requests.

If you predominantly prefer one representational system, you'll likely communicate in that way. You can miss out on building rapport if the other person has a different preferred representational system. Once you know your preferred representational system, you can become more conscious of communicating in other representational systems, focusing on how they like to communicate.

Understanding and communicating in another person's preferred representational systems leads to better relationships and reduced misunderstandings.

Reference: Heslin, D. *NLP Practitioner Manual.* Debra Heslin Wellness, Inc. Link to NLP Practitioner Training https://www.debraheslinwellness.com/nlp-certification

THE 4-MAT SYSTEM

Do you find it challenging to communicate a new idea effectively? Are you unsure how to structure your presentation?

Quiet Achievers generally do not enjoy being on show and the centre of attention. There are many times in our careers when we must clearly articulate our thoughts. The 4-MAT system is a game changer, providing a structured approach to planning your message. This system is ideal for teaching new techniques, introducing new ideas or building presentations. It helps you organise information, stay focused and communicate your message with precision.

Using the 4-MAT system to structure your communication makes it easier for others to understand and relate to you, as they will perceive that you know what you are talking about.

Using the 4-MAT system is easy and takes away any anxiety when it comes to being in the spotlight communicating your message.

When explaining things using the 4-MAT system, incorporate Visual, Auditory and Kinaesthetic (VAK) elements. Here are a few examples of common words and phrases to use.

VISUAL	AUDITORY	KINAESTHETIC
See, Look, Illuminate, Clear, Imagine, Crystal, Picture	Hear, Listen, In tune, Be heard, Sounds	Feel, Touch, Grasp, Make contact, Get a handle
You will see	Clear as a bell	Come to grips with
Appears to me	Hidden message	Pull some strings
In light of	State your purpose	Start from scratch
Looks like	Tuned in/tuned out	Get in touch with
Paint a picture	Word for word	Hang in there

Simply put, the 4-MAT system consists of structuring your message as follows;

1. WHY
2. WHAT
3. HOW
4. WHAT IF

The following image outlines what to cover in each section.

REMEMBER – always structure your message in the same order – 1, 2, 3, 4.

Start in the top right-hand quadrant (1), move clockwise finishing in the top left-hand quadrant (4).

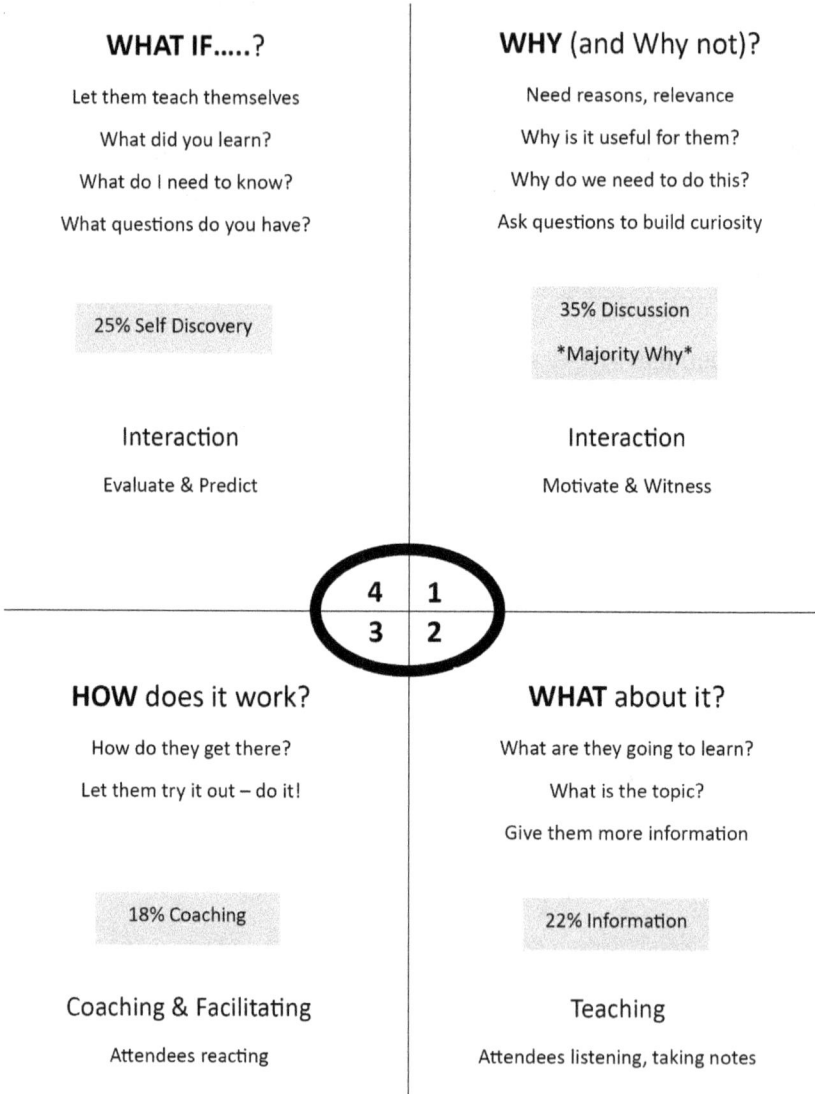

WHAT IF.....?	**WHY** (and Why not)?
Let them teach themselves	Need reasons, relevance
What did you learn?	Why is it useful for them?
What do I need to know?	Why do we need to do this?
What questions do you have?	Ask questions to build curiosity
25% Self Discovery	35% Discussion *Majority Why*
Interaction	Interaction
Evaluate & Predict	Motivate & Witness

4	1
3	2

HOW does it work?	**WHAT** about it?
How do they get there?	What are they going to learn?
Let them try it out – do it!	What is the topic?
	Give them more information
18% Coaching	22% Information
Coaching & Facilitating	Teaching
Attendees reacting	Attendees listening, taking notes

Reference: *Heslin, D. The FasTrak Neuro-Linguistic Programming Master Practitioner Certification Training Manual.* Debra Heslin Wellness, Inc. Link to NLP Master Practitioner Training https://www.debraheslinwellness.com

4-MAT EXAMPLE

I wrote an article titled 'The Path to Discovery Starts With You: Melissa's Journey to Self-Discovery' for the Beam Magazine. You can find the article at www.beammagazine.com and selecting my name on the left-hand side.

Below I have provided a brief outline of how the article was structured using the 4-MAT system.

TOPIC

The Path to Discovery Starts With You: Melissa's Journey to Self-Discovery

WHY
- Tired of being controlled by the constraints of a large organisation
- Tired of typical Monday to Friday work week
- Quit my job to take time for me and travel
- I wanted to help others make the changes they desired in their lives

WHAT
- Owned my own bullshit and learned lessons
- Change starts with you
- Look inward and own your truth
- Be led by your soul

HOW
- Living my dream life
- Wrote my second book, the one you are reading
- Coaching others through my business, Integrated Soul

WHAT IF

- You found this same sense of purpose and fulfilment in your own life
- Are you on the right path?
- Are you on a journey that truly belongs to you, or are you following someone else's path?
- Are you where you genuinely wish to be?

PREPARATION IS KEY

Preparation is key to making a lasting impression. Quiet Achievers thrive when they have ample time to gather their thoughts and ideas. Take the initiative to prepare for meetings, presentations and any situation where you want to be heard. By coming into a discussion or project well-prepared, you'll be more confident and able to convey your message clearly and concisely.

Preparation Tips:

- Review the agenda prior to the event or meeting
- Prepare thoughts on the topics
- Anticipate questions
- Identify personal stories related to the topic
- Mentally prepare – use the 4-MAT system
- Get into state before event or meeting

Quiet Achievers can be perceived as lacking input and contribution due to needing time to process and reflect on the information being presented. Quiet Achievers typically only speak to offer an opinion or suggestion if they believe it adds genuine value. If you are still processing and reflecting on the information being presented, consider asking clarifying questions during meetings or events to ensure meaningful involvement. Be honest and upfront about needing time to reflect, and commit to providing input later.

Communicating personal stories builds a stronger presence professionally. What personal stories do you have to share related to the topic? What were the achievements, challenges and learnings? Highlight the impact of your contributions and share why, what and how you made a difference to the outcome. Craft your story so it is relatable to the audience using simple, clear language. Sharing your challenges and failures makes your story more compelling and helps those listening avoid the same pitfalls.

STATE OF BEING

Be authentic when conveying messages, whether you're interacting with work colleagues or leaders. Any deviation or distortion in messaging undermines our integrity as it compromises our authenticity and being true to ourselves.

Be open and curious. I've discovered the more open I am, the more I recognise how much I have yet to learn. Approaching situations with openness, exploration, and curiosity enables a broader perspective. It's akin to having peripheral vision rather than tunnel vision, expanding your awareness beyond your immediate surroundings. This expanded perspective provides a sense of freedom and choice, empowering you to feel in control of your decisions and fostering stability and security.

I focus on achieving a centred state before undertaking any task. Some may call it a grounded state. Getting into this state is a simple process:

take a few deep breaths, relax your mind and body, and visualise roots extending down into the ground while feeling connected to the sky above. You can also move your arms/body and set an intention by stating, either mentally or verbally, what you wish to accomplish during the meeting or task. I often ask the universe for assistance, and you can ask whoever or whatever represents a higher being to you. This practice has been a game changer for me, and it is so simple and quick.

CULTIVATE CONNECTIONS, FOSTER SUPPORT, EXPAND YOUR NETWORK

Cultivate connections, foster supporters, and expand your network. Approach it by asking:

"How can I add value? How can I support you?"

Build relationships focused on how you can add value rather than what you can receive. Often, we approach networking with a mindset of personal gain, which can feel selfish and transactional. By focusing on giving, relationships thrive more successfully.

Be fair and consistent. Treat everyone equally and hold them to the same standard. Avoid being wishy-washy, where you demand quality one moment and settle for less the next. Inconsistency only creates confusion. By maintaining a steady output and reliable delivery, people will recognise and value your consistency, leading to appreciation and acknowledgment.

Take the time to connect with others. Focus on meaningful, one-on-one conversations rather than larger group interactions. After meeting someone, follow up with a personal message or email to show genuine interest. Find out what their interests are, what they are doing in their time away from work. Extend well wishes for their activities and enquire about their time off and experiences afterward. Engage in casual conversation at the beginning of the work week or roster, asking about their time off, family, pets or other interests. Most people enjoy discussing their passions, so finding their interests and asking questions demonstrates genuine care and interest.

Utilise online platforms. Does your organisation have a messaging application? Can you message with other sites or departments? Find your counterpart. Utilise LinkedIn. Share articles, comment on posts and engage in industry-specific discussions. Join Facebook groups and professional groups related to your area of expertise. Participate in discussions and share your knowledge.

Look out for smaller, more focused networking events and workshops. Go with a friend, colleague or another business owner. Recently I went with another business owner to a networking event. Going together helped us both get out of our comfort zones. Look for breakout sessions or smaller group discussions at larger conferences where you can engage more comfortably.

Have individuals you already know introduce you to other connections. This can happen via email, introduction calls or in person.

Volunteer for cross-departmental projects or communities within your organisation. This allows you to work with colleagues from different areas. Get involved in professional associations or community groups/ events. Ask your organisation to support a selected charity or fundraiser and ask your colleagues to join the team. I recently did this at my workplace to support the Royal Flying Doctors. As team members, we had to commit to a dollar amount we would raise and the distance we would walk for the chosen month. My workplace even matched dollar for dollar and we all improved our fitness.

Listen to what others say and ask further questions to understand their perspective. People feel appreciated when they are heard and understood.

TOP FIVE

Who are your Top Five? Think about the major goals you are working towards. Identify five individuals who can help you achieve these goals. Before you start the cogs turning, it is not your family or loved ones. Their role is often to keep you safe and protect you from potential pitfalls as you strive for your goals. Let them fulfil that role.

Your Top Five could include:

- Someone who is or could be a good coach for you
- Someone who is or could be a good mentor for you
- Someone you can model
- Someone who is a trusted colleague
- Someone who can teach you the specific skills you need to achieve your goal
- Someone who is already doing what you want to achieve
- Someone who has a community linked to what you do or want to achieve and can help you get recognised

Start brainstorming your Top Five now! You may already have some or all of your Top Five in your life! If you can't list specific people, list what you need in the individual and go looking for the right person. Nurture your relationship with your Top Five.

MY TOP FIVE

1. _____
2. _____
3. _____
4. _____
5. _____

INNOVATION AND CONTINUOUS IMPROVEMENT

Emphasising innovation and continuous improvement is necessary for enhancing performance. As a Quiet Achiever, I have found it challenging around innovation and continuous improvement to share the changes made and the successes achieved through these alterations. It can feel like you are promoting oneself and one's efforts, whether they involve product enhancements, service improvements or subtle workplace adjustments.

Sharing your innovations can be done through various channels, such as discussing them with peers or colleagues during informal conversations, perhaps in the break room. Sometimes, even overhearing someone else's challenges presents an opportunity to join the dialogue and share your experiences, whether positive or negative. When it comes to the negatives, it's important to reflect on how you've grown from them, turning them into positive takeaways. This applies to not only your current workplace but also to past experiences. Share what strategies have been effective and what haven't. It's essential to recognise that innovation doesn't always require monumental leaps; small changes and incremental improvements are equally significant.

I recall a situation where a colleague sought advice on managing a difficult team member and they were struggling with performance tracking and performance review processes. I took this chance to share my approach, detailing how I tracked my team member's performance, conducted regular check-ins with team members and facilitated performance reviews. By providing insights into and sharing my spreadsheet template and coaching methods, I enabled them to adapt these practices to their own style. Months later, they reported back on how much smoother their team performance and review processes had become after implementing these habits and changes.

Regular conversations are vital because they often lead to solutions for challenges that seem insurmountable. Once you connect and chat, you may also find they have the exact solution you need. As a Quiet Achiever, failing to share your knowledge and expertise with others is a disservice to those around you, as they may benefit greatly from your insights and experiences. In essence, by sharing your strategies and accomplishments, it can spark new ideas and you contribute to the collective growth and success of your team and organisation. Openly sharing learnings demonstrates transparency and builds trust among team members. I've never enjoyed that feeling of restriction in my throat when I haven't shared my knowledge. It feels so much better to share and be heard.

Continuously review and improve how you work. Review the processes, systems, policies and procedures within your work area, as there's always room for improvement. An example of this is my return to the same organisation after a decade, where I identified numerous changes to streamline tasks and make the job easier. I scratched my head why these changes were not identified during my initial employment. This highlights the importance of critical thinking and constantly seeking better approaches.

When implementing changes, evaluate their effectiveness. Avoid implementing successive changes without allowing time for the previous ones to embed and assess their impact. Change management is intricate and can evoke strong emotions in individuals. Excessive changes without adequate time for adaptation and review can create a sense of chaos and instability, especially for Quiet Achievers who prefer consistency. It's crucial to communicate the rationale behind the changes to ensure understanding and support. Make sure the change has a compelling why that is communicated to motivate the team to take action and adopt the change.

Engage those familiar with the job to identify pain points and participate in continuous improvement and review processes. Never undertake these tasks in isolation.

Always learn and improve. Quiet Achievers who seek knowledge and skill enhancement are valuable resources in their organisations. Showcase your commitment to self-improvement to make you more visible to those who value growth and development.

CELEBRATE SUCCESS

Quiet Achievers often prefer low-key celebrations of their success, valuing genuine recognition versus elaborate fanfare. They appreciate acknowledgment in a more subtle and meaningful way.

As a leader, I had to learn to stop and celebrate my team's successes. I was often so focused on our objectives that even after reaching a major milestone, despite my pride and gratitude for their efforts, I would quickly move on to the next goal.

Consider hosting a celebration, whether it's with a cake, a barbecue, a gift, an event outside of work or another enjoyable activity. Express gratitude to those who contributed to your success by saying thank you and recognising their support.

Celebrating success:

- Generates positive feelings, builds confidence and reinforces the individual's value
- Increases visibility by highlighting contributions
- Sets a precedent, encouraging continuous improvement and future achievements
- Fosters a sense of belonging
- Builds stronger connections with others
- Recognises the input of others who have helped you succeed

A simple way to celebrate success is get everyone to share their wins at the start of a regular e.g. weekly meeting. Try it! Notice how it sets a positive energy for the meeting and fosters team support. Everyone has a win to share, whether it is big or small.

CHAPTER 3

DEVELOP BULLETPROOF, SELF-BELIEF AND SPEAK UP CONFIDENTLY EVERY TIME

3 DEVELOP BULLETPROOF, SELF-BELIEF AND SPEAK UP CONFIDENTLY EVERY TIME

"Trust yourself. You know more than you think you do."
Dr Benjamin Spock

In the past, I've struggled with speaking up confidently when I doubted my competence, even though I often possessed the necessary skills; it was self-belief I lacked.

Yet I've seen the most innovative ideas emerge from individuals who, despite lacking expertise, approach a topic with a fresh perspective. I've witnessed this phenomenon numerous times in my work, such as when visitors to the lab or colleagues in discussions proposed alternative approaches. Each of us brings a unique contribution shaped by our diverse backgrounds, experiences, knowledge, values and beliefs.

If others who lack competence can offer great ideas confidently, then developing bulletproof self-belief is the key for consistently speaking up with confidence.

BUILD YOUR BULLETPROOF SELF-BELIEF

1. **Reflect on past successes**

    Make a list of all the problems you have solved and your past successes at work. Keep going until you have one hundred items on your list. One hundred items requires deeper reflection and helps us access the memories stored in our unconscious mind.

Reflecting on past successes and problem-solving abilities reframes self-doubt, bolsters confidence and resourcefulness. The key is to be resourceful. There's always a solution; be persistent.

ACTIVITY Make a list of one hundred problems you have solved at work. Keep going until you have one hundred!

2. Mentor/Train others

Teaching others solidifies your understanding and expertise. Receiving positive feedback and appreciation from mentees/trainees reinforces your value and skills. Seeing others grow and learn due to your support highlights your impact. Mentoring/Training prompts you to reflect on your journey and accomplishments helping you realise how much you do know, reinforcing your belief in your capabilities.

3. Step out of your comfort zone

---

*"When you are asked if you can do
a job, tell 'em, Certainly I can!
Then get busy and find out how to do it."*
Theodore Roosevelt

Challenge yourself by taking on new tasks or projects that push you out of your comfort zone. Focus on your unique insights and value you bring. Develop new skills and gain exposure in areas where you may not have previously been recognised. Break larger objectives into smaller, achievable tasks. Celebrate each small success to build momentum, self-belief and confidence.

Stepping outside your comfort zone feels uncomfortable. Embrace the discomfort! You will learn what you need surprisingly quickly and be able to take the next step. It's a great way to build resilience and self-belief.

We often say we are nervous when we are attempting something new and stepping out of our comfort zone. I now reframe this nervous feeling and call it excitement. I'm excited to do something new and find out what there is to learn.

Nervousness = Excitement

---

4. **Notice your self-talk**

What are you telling yourself? Are you using positive or negative language? Are you focused on what you want or what you lack? You'll attract more of what you focus on.

"Whether you think you can or you think you can't, you're right."
Henry Ford

My coach played a crucial role in helping me recognise my language patterns. She pointed out when I was being negative or using limiting statements. I often said, "I'm trying", which is a negative phrase that held me back from fully achieving my goals.

Words that may indicate negative suggestions are being used:

Try	Maybe	Hope	Should
Never	Don't	Can't	

Words that may indicate positive suggestions are being used:

Succeed	Will	Know
Always	Do	Can

5. Clear the junk in the trunk

We often carry negative emotions/thoughts, foster limiting beliefs and decisions that hinder us from achieving our goals. Many of us continue living this way without realising how it affects our thoughts, dialogue and behaviours. To achieve our desired outcomes, we need to clear the junk in the trunk. Another way of saying it is, "we need to let go of our excess baggage".

The gold nugget for me in developing bulletproof self-belief has been working with a Neuro-Linguistic Programming (NLP)-trained coach to clear the junk in my trunk. My experience with NLP coaching has been life changing, leading to immediate desired behavioural changes through effortless techniques.

NLP is a psychological approach that explores the connections between neurological processes (neuro), language (linguistic), and behavioural patterns learned through experience (programming). NLP is how to use the language of the mind to consistently achieve our specific and desired outcomes. All you need is a desire to change and a willingness to understand and improve how you think, communicate and behave.

Some NLP concepts that help build self-belief:

- Anchoring – associating positive emotions with specific triggers to access a specific state (e.g. confidence) when needed
- Visualisation – creating vivid mental images of successful outcomes to boost self-belief
- Reframing – changing negative thoughts into positive perspectives to alter limiting beliefs
- Swish Patterns – replacing unwanted behaviours or thoughts with desired ones by visualisation
- Meta-Model – challenging and clarifying limiting language patterns to uncover underlying beliefs
- Submodalities - altering the qualities of mental images (like brightness or size) to change emotional responses
- Positive Self-Talk – using positive language to reinforce confidence

I was so gobsmacked by the effortless way NLP allows us to clear our junk that I became a NLP Master Practitioner to use these NLP techniques with my coaching clients. If you're interested in becoming NLP-trained, check out Debra Heslin and her NLP training offerings at https://www.debraheslinwellness.com/ . Other modalities such as Timeline Therapy and Hypnosis are also covered in NLP training.

I love watching my clients light-up during our coaching or personal breakthrough sessions as their neurology transforms and they clear their excess baggage. They literally glow, as if they've just had a makeover. If you are wanting to make a change, book a FREE Insight Call with me to discuss how I can help you clear your junk in your trunk, and help you with that change.

https://integratedsoul.com.au/services/insight-call/

APPROACH EVERYTHING WITH AN OPEN MIND

"Assume nothing, question everything."
James Patterson

In my younger days, both as a leader and in my personal relationships, I frequently made assumptions about my team members and others, presuming I understood their situations. My intentions were well-meaning, aimed at offering assistance. I was often surprised during conversations with them by gaining insight into their perspectives. I am deeply grateful for all the valuable lessons my team members and relationships have taught me.

Now I consciously pause to challenge any assumptions I may be forming. I've adopted a habit of questioning everything, recognising the more I question, the more I learn. I firmly believe everyone has the answers within them, and it is through questioning that these insights emerge.

Approach problems with an open mind. Refrain from setting the solution or outcome before asking questions. Fully engage in exploring all possibilities, thinking innovatively without being constrained by preconceived notions. Play full out. Think outside the box. This mindset ensures that you're not limiting potential solutions and opportunities that may be beyond your current perception.

> *"It's easier to think outside the box if you don't draw one around yourself."*
> **Jason Kravitz**

Asking questions builds self-belief by:

- Encouraging critical thinking
- Identifying what truly matters, leading to more focused efforts
- Finding solutions to problems
- Learning from experiences

"Telephone did not come into existence from the persistent improvement of the postcard."
Amit Kalantri

DECISION-MAKING STRATEGY

To have bulletproof self-belief, you must be confident in making decisions.

Do you go round and round in circles before you make a decision?

Do you know what information you need to help you make a decision?

Did you know we each have our own strategy for making decisions?

Everything we do involves strategies. All our daily activities are generated and maintained by strategies. We have strategies for everything we do, for example, love, wealth, making decisions, eating, relaxation, communication, health, sex, fun, procrastination, overwhelm, talking and everything else. Whether or not we finish what we do is governed by a strategy.

When we were young, we learned to make decisions by linking an internal and external experience, followed by making a decision. This process forms a strategy consisting of specific steps for decision-making. Your decision-making strategy may be efficient or inefficient. For instance, you may easily prioritise weekend tasks but struggle with prioritising work tasks, indicating different strategies for each area.

For me, discovering my decision-making strategy was a breakthrough. It explained why I sometimes go in circles trying to decide - I didn't have the necessary information I needed to complete the steps in my decision-making strategy sequence. Understanding what information you need helps you make decisions more quickly and confidently, enhancing self-belief.

A strategy is a specific sequence of external and internal representations that consistently leads to a specific outcome. Everything we experience is dictated by a series of steps (made up of external and internal representations) that run in the same sequence every time.

A strategy has the following three essential components:

1. The Outcome
2. The Elements
3. The Sequence

For simplicity, in terms of the elements we will use Visual, Auditory, Kinaesthetic and Auditory Digital.

VISUAL	AUDITORY	KINAESTHETIC	AUDITORY DIGITAL
Pictures	Sounds	Feelings	Makes sense
Look	Told	Touch	Talk to yourself
Something you saw	Something you heard	Touch of someone or something	Understand
Way someone looked at you	Someone's tone of voice		Experience
			Consider the value

Reference: Heslin, D. *NLP Practitioner Manual.* Debra Heslin Wellness, Inc. Link to NLP Practitioner Training https://www.debraheslinwellness.com/nlp-certification

So, how do you work out what your decision-making strategy is?

ACTIVITY Determine your decision-making strategy

The first step in determining your decision-making strategy is to think of a specific time when you felt confident making a decision. An easy example is to think of a time when you felt confident purchasing an item.

My specific time was when I purchased a small garden tool.

Ask yourself, "What was the very first thing that happened so you knew that was the item for you?"

The first thing that happened for me was how the garden tool **looked**. The first step in my decision-making strategy is **Visual**.

V

Ask yourself, "After you (saw, heard, felt) that, what was the very next thing that happened so you knew that was the item for you?"

The second thing that happened for me was how the garden tool **felt** in my hand.

The second step in my decision-making strategy is **Kinaesthetic**.

V ➡ K

Ask yourself, "After you (saw, heard, felt) that, what was the very next thing that happened so you knew that was the item for you?"

The third thing that happened for me was I started **talking to myself** and comparing the prices of my favourite garden tools considering the **best value** for the quality of the garden tool. I decided my preferred garden tool.

The third step in my decision-making strategy is **Auditory Digital**.

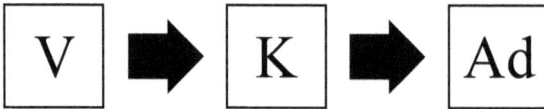

$$V \Rightarrow K \Rightarrow Ad$$

Ask yourself, "After you (saw, heard, felt) that, what was the very next thing that happened so you knew that was the item for you?" Continue until complete.

The fourth thing that happened for me was I **visually** inspected all the available garden tools of my preferred type and I chose the 'best of the bunch'.

The fourth step in my decision-making strategy is **Visual**.

$$V \Rightarrow K \Rightarrow Ad \Rightarrow V$$

Off I went to purchase the 'best' garden tool, confident I had made a good decision.

So this tells me what information I need in what sequence to feel confident when making decisions.

Your decision-making strategy may have less steps than mine. There is no right or wrong.

If your decision-making strategy is inefficient, a NLP trained coach can help you change your strategy and once your new strategy is designed, can help you install it so that it becomes natural and automatic.

Strategies are effective when utilised correctly. When helping a client make the change they desire, I elicit the presenting root problem and the strategy for the root problem and then we install the new strategy to achieve the desired change. It's very cool!

TRUST YOUR INTUITION (GUT FEEL)

At some point between my twenties and thirties, I chose to disconnect from and ignore my intuition. I believed my analytical and logical mind knew best, often over-relying on it. It wasn't until my late thirties that I began to listen to my intuition again, and only in my forties did I start to trust it again. My intuition was always trying to reach me but I would shove those messages and feelings back down, preferring not to pay attention.

In 2015, I was diagnosed with ovarian cancer and that was a pivotal moment for me. It made me realise that significant aspects of my life were out of whack. Our intuition is the way our soul communicates with us. I was shoving down so deeply, what my soul was trying to convey to me, my soul had to create cancer to wake me up. Cancer has been a profound gift.

I now combine intuition with rational thinking to make balanced decisions and take action. I reach a point of inner knowing that it's the right choice, and even if I feel uncertain, I keep moving forward, taking action. A great way to build bulletproof self-belief. It always turns out better than relying on logic alone.

How does your intuition get your attention?

Is it a gut feeling?

Is it a subtle or fleeting thought?

Is it a physical sensation in your body?

If you are where I was, relying on logic alone, this is how I started to combine intuition with logical thinking to make balanced decisions.

1. Identify a decision you need to make

2. List all your options, writing each one on a separate sticky note

3. Place the sticky notes on the floor with space between them

4. Choose one sticky note (option) and stand on it

5. Close your eyes and breathe until you feel calm

6. Focus on your mind and ask what it thinks about this option

7. Then, shift your attention to where you feel centred – perhaps your heart or gut. Ask your soul/intuition how it feels about this option.

Can you sense the difference between your logical thinking and intuition? Often the two aren't aligned, and it's important to honour both. They each play a part in protecting and supporting you. Find a compromise until they come into alignment.

For example, my soul urged me to leap and quit my job, suggesting everything would work out, and my logical thinking thought it was crazy and suggested staying for financial security. In the end, the compromise was to set a timeframe for how long I could be unemployed by assessing my finances. This approach satisfied my need for security while giving me the freedom my soul desired. It turned out better than expected, my employer offered to hold my position for twelve months. Ultimately, I didn't return, but it was a great compromise between logic and intuition. If I had only listened to my logical thinking, I would have continued in the job.

You may experience discomfort and confusion before reaching alignment. Lean in! When the right choice appears, the confusion will vanish, replaced by clarity.

Trust your intuition by:

- Paying attention to the feelings, sensations and instincts that arise without overthinking
- Noticing any recurring feelings, sensations or thoughts that are guiding you
- Quieting your mind through meditation or deep breathing to hear your intuition
- Making smaller decisions based on combined logical thinking and intuition to build confidence
- Believing you make the right choices when combining logical thinking and intuition

A trained NLP coach can help you reach alignment (integration) if you're facing issues where one part of you wants one thing and another part wants something else. They can assist in overcoming resistance and integrating your desires.

CHAPTER 4

SHINE BRIGHT AND NOT BURN OUT

4 SHINE BRIGHT AND NOT BURN OUT

RECOGNISING THE SIGNS OF BURNOUT

Quiet Achievers are at risk of burnout because they may accept additional work without setting boundaries, can feel undervalued due to lack of recognition, avoid asking for help and their high standards can lead to overwork and exhaustion.

"If you feel 'burnout' setting in, if you feel demoralised and exhausted, it is best, for the sake of everyone, to withdraw and restore yourself."
Dalai Lama

Ideally, we want to avoid burnout. If you notice any of these behaviours in yourself, it's time to pause and assess what's going on:

- Feeling drained or overwhelmed
- Headaches, muscle tension, disturbed sleep or frequent illness
- Decline in productivity or effectiveness at work
- Decreased enthusiasm or motivation for tasks you once enjoyed
- Increased negativity or detachment from work or colleagues
- Increased frustration with work colleagues or loved ones
- Difficulty focusing or making decisions
- Withdrawing from team activities or social interactions

"Life is a gift – Choose you, shine bright and live your best life."
Melissa Haggarty

TIME MANAGEMENT – IDEAL WEEK

I believe I have ample time to accomplish everything. In the past I procrastinated by not focusing on the right tasks that achieved the results I wanted. That changed once I implemented my ideal week. Initially, when I began utilising my ideal week, the rigour of the discipline taught me to create habits that became routine.

"Lack of direction, not lack of time, is the problem. We all have twenty-four-hour days."
Zig Ziglar

Make a list of tasks you need to complete in your week.

For example: Exercise, Meal Prep, Emails, Urgent Actions, Accounts, Social Media, Meetings, Networking, Research and Development, Customer Relations, Product/Service Build, Family Commitments, Free Time for changes and unknown tasks.

How does your ideal schedule work? Do you follow it weekly or alternate between two weeks? Do you have a specific roster? Create a template for your schedule using half-hour time blocks.

Start by filling in these time blocks, including daily 'free time' with nothing planned. Limit each activity block to a maximum of ninety minutes, followed by a quick break. Colour code your activities, use the same colour for the same activity.

Once your ideal week is set, focus on the scheduled tasks. If new tasks arise, add them to your to-do list. Use your free time or dedicate time each day to address these tasks.

Remember your ideal week is exactly that – 'ideal'! There will be times when it will go off track. It will be OK – the world will not end.

If your ideal week is not working, change it.

THE ONE THING

"Focus is a matter of deciding what things you're not going to do."
John Carmack

Now that I've introduced the concept of your ideal week, I want to shake it up. I want each day to start with time allocated to your 'ONE thing'.

"What's the ONE thing you can do this week such that by doing it everything else would be easier or unnecessary?"

Reference: Gary Keller with Jay Papasan (2019). *The One Thing – The Surprisingly Simple Truth Behind Extraordinary Results.* John Murry Learning.

Go back to your ideal week. Move things around to make time for your ONE thing at the start of the day. Get your ONE thing done!

ACTIVITY Build your ideal week by using the template at https://integratedsoul.com.au/books/quiet-achievers/

MANAGING NEW ROLES, ADDITIONAL PROJECTS AND DEADLINES

When taking on a new role or additional projects, clarify the purpose behind doing so. For individuals who excel at achieving quietly, it's easy to become overwhelmed with an ever-growing workload. Therefore, when faced with extra tasks, it's important to evaluate the benefits of completing them and not simply say yes out of obligation. Ensure that the work aligns strategically with your goals, whether it involves acquiring new skills, collaborating with different individuals, or expanding your knowledge and confirm that it fits within your existing workload.

While there may be instances when stretching yourself to take on extra work is worth the effort for personal growth, it's essential to recognise when it becomes the norm and to speak up when necessary. If you find yourself overloaded with too many priorities, initiate a conversation about what can be reprioritised or delegated. I wasted time stressing about meeting certain deadlines, trying to keep all the balls in the air and losing sleep over how I was going to achieve it all. Drawing from personal experience, I've learned the importance of understanding the rationale behind priorities and deadlines. While some deadlines may be flexible, others are non-negotiable.

For instance, during the commissioning of a LNG plant, my team and I were responsible for ensuring product quality for the first shipment. This was a non-negotiable deliverable. There were years of scoping and commissioning activities that had been completed to successfully meet this critical deadline. A week before the scheduled ship arrival, my team and I were summoned to the general manager's office to ensure readiness to deliver the expected product quality for the first cargo shipment. We were asked if we had completed all necessary preparations and if there were any potential obstacles to success. We assured him we were fully prepared and confident in our abilities.

As the deadline approached, the pressure mounted, particularly as it coincided with New Year's Eve and we encountered difficulties maintaining sufficient pressure in the line to obtain a sample. The management and operations team celebrated on the mainland, leaving only the construction crew on site. Despite reassurances from the operations manager that day that estimating the product quality would suffice in the absence of actual analysis, I remained sceptical, given the stringent requirements outlined in our cargo agreements. Many hours had been spent with the commercial teams and the ship surveyors cross-checking our calculations and analysis processes to ensure we met the specifications of the cargo agreements. I sought assistance from a construction manager on site, without whom we wouldn't have succeeded in troubleshooting obtaining the sample.

Ultimately, my understanding that it was a non-negotiable deadline proved right when, on Friday morning, I received confirmation that actual analysis was indeed necessary. Gratefully, I had persevered in delivering on our commitments.

PLAN HOLIDAYS

Are you aware of your annual leave entitlement? Do you have clarity on any special leave allowances, such as volunteering days? Do you actively plan your holidays, whether they be extended breaks or short getaways? Familiarise yourself with the leave policy and procedures within your organisation. Understand how your team manages leave assignments and approvals, and the criteria for shift rostering if applicable. It's important to adhere to established rules and plan your leave in advance. Remember, the work will continue in your absence, and someone else may temporarily fill your role. Upon your return, there may be tasks to catch up on, but prioritise and refocus accordingly.

I've participated in commissioning and setting up laboratories across four diverse industries. In some cases these organisations had blackout periods during which employees couldn't take leave, whether due to specific milestones in the commissioning process or during plant shutdowns. If your organisation has similar policies in place, it highlights the importance of carefully planning your breaks and leave periods.

USE PERSONAL (SICK) LEAVE

Staying in the same job for thirty years was the norm for my father's generation. He dedicated three decades to working for Ansett before Ansett's collapse left him unemployed. His parenting instilled in me the importance of valuing and safeguarding one's job, especially if it offered good pay and was with a reputable company. Consequently, I internalised the notion of not taking sick leave as a means of looking after my job.

Early in my career, I adhered to this mindset, often showing up to work even when unwell and potentially passing what I had onto others in the workplace. Looking back, I realised that I could have recovered from illnesses much faster had I allowed myself time to rest. There was an instance after attending the Gympie music muster where I fell ill due to food poisoning on my birthday. I remember talking to my Dad later that night for my birthday, telling him I had the day off work because I was unwell. Even though I explained I couldn't go to work because I was spewing my guts up, his primary concern appeared to be for my job security rather than my well-being.

However, everything changed when I met one of my partners, who taught me not to martyr myself and to utilise my sick leave when necessary. This marked a significant shift in my approach to work, as I began listening to my body and prioritising self-care. It was empowering to acknowledge that it's okay to prioritise my own well-being.

Moreover, I discovered that work could function smoothly in my absence and that any issues arising from my leave could be resolved afterward. This realisation liberated me from the guilt associated with taking time off and reinforced the importance of self-care in maintaining overall productivity and well-being.

CHOOSE YOUR BATTLES

Understand you can't win every war. Be selective about when to engage in battle. It involves confidently expressing your viewpoints backed by solid evidence, and if you don't succeed initially, persevere if it's a cause worth fighting for. Often the timing of the fight is critical.

I had a team member wanting to apply for a part-time flexible work arrangement following their return from parental leave. The policy stated if the request was denied, the applicant had to wait twelve months to reapply. The organisation was going through significant change and I advised my team member I believed if they applied for a flexible work arrangement at this time, it would be denied. My manager indicated his agreement.

It was challenging to accept that we had to wait when the policy was in place for such arrangements; however it was a battle I could not win, at that time, in that environment.

I suggested we spend time looking at solutions to cover the other portion of the flexible working arrangement to build a solid case. The team member applied when the organisational change was complete and the flexible working arrangement was approved and implemented.

HEALTHY ROUTINES

I've noticed common traits among many successful CEOs of companies. They appear well put-together individuals. They are organised, physically fit, active, and adept at giving and receiving quick feedback, all indicators of having everything under control.

Healthy routines play a significant role in this. Healthy routines involve discipline and consistency. Without these elements, achieving progress becomes challenging.

What does your morning routine look like?

My morning routine includes moving my body - a walk or gym session, journaling and setting my intentions for the day.

I recently joined VibeFit, a local small group strength training studio, and signed up for semi-private personal training sessions. What I love most is the absence of mirrors; perfect for a Quiet Achiever. Instead of relying on mirrors, you focus on how the exercise feels to ensure proper form. It's important to find the right place or group where you enjoy working out, and that tailors their programs to fit your individual needs. VibeFit is featured in the Resources section in the back of the book as they also offer lifestyle and nutrition coaching, corporate wellness programs and online options.

Journaling has made a massive difference in my world. I dedicate one of my journals solely to gratitude and curiosity, allowing me to focus on these two areas. I no longer worry if I don't have the answers I need. This is my process for handing the questions over to the universe. It makes life so simple as the answers are then provided at the right time. In my journal on a single page, I write:

The Date _____

Grateful For:

List the things I'm grateful for _____

_____

_____

_____

_____

_____

Curious About:

List the questions I need answers for _____

_____

_____

_____

_____

_____

I absolutely love my journal and feel excited when I open it up to write in it. Use it as an opportunity to choose a journal you absolutely love and then it ramps up the pleasure.

Other ideas for healthy routines are:

- Visualisations
- Meditations
- Reading
- Podcasts
- Silence
- Deep breathing
- Draw oracle cards

DECLUTTER HOUSE AND WORKSPACE

What does your space at home and work look like? Is it organised? Is it messy? Is it cluttered? Is there clear space? I find my space at home and work always reflects how I feel inside. If I feel overwhelmed, my space will look chaotic and disorganised. If I feel calm, my space will look clean and organised. The reverse also works, often I have to clean and declutter my space to set the tone for how I want to feel inside. Save time by organising what you have so it is easier to find. A clean, organised space improves your overall mood. We don't realise how heavy clutter is energetically until we sort it and remove it and feel the relief and freedom of clear space. This takes care of clearing the physical clutter.

What about clearing energetic clutter? When I first moved in to my new home, the house felt stagnant and stuck. I'd been in my new home for twelve months and energetically I was feeling stuck, looping in procrastination. I was specifically feeling stuck in taking action towards making my new home feel like mine. I saw a Facebook post advertising Land Healings by Hayley Wallace and enquired. Hayley advised there could be earth energies, energies from past residents and energies in the home that could still be present and impacting me. I said yes to a Land Healing!

Hayley identified all of the challenges, present energies, performed energy healing work on my home and land. She provided a map with specific crystals and instructions where they needed to be placed to help balance the energies.

Since doing a Land Healing with Hayley, I have noticed a change in how I feel on my land and in my home. There is a sense of calm and lightness as confirmation of the energetic declutter. I am excited about renovating my new home.

Land Healings by Hayley Wallace is featured in the Resources section in the back of the book.

LEAVE WORK AT WORK

On the last day of each work week I had a standing appointment titled 'Lab Meeting' scheduled for two hours every Friday. While it may have appeared to others as a meeting with the lab team, it was dedicated time for me. During this period I would prepare for the upcoming week, reviewing priorities, rearranging meetings, and mentally organising tasks. It served as a time to address any outstanding issues, such as responding to emails or following up on messages, ensuring that loose ends were tied up before the weekend.

This ritual of sorting, closing out, and organising provided me with a sense of clarity and peace of mind. It allowed me to leave for my scheduled days off without any lingering concerns, knowing that everything had been addressed or appropriately scheduled for the following week. Additionally, if there were any pressing matters causing anxiety or concern, I could outline actions to address them in the coming week.

The meeting time was only broken in the event of a genuine emergency, such as a site or production crisis requiring immediate attention from the laboratory.

At the end of each day, I would do a mental dump of the tasks on my mind. I would add them to my action list. I was fortunate to have a twenty-minute drive home from work and during this time I would consciously relax and switch my focus to being present when I walked through my front door. Playing my favourite music on the way home is always a winning strategy.

WHEN IT STOPS WORKING - MOVE ON

When you find yourself heading towards burnout it's crucial to assess whether you're in the right environment for your well-being. While earning income is essential for survival and enables us to pursue activities we enjoy, it's equally important to evaluate the toll our work environment may be taking on us. Reflect on how you're navigating your work tasks—are you being authentic, speaking up when necessary, saying no when needed and maintaining productivity?

Additionally, consider whether the expectations placed on you are reasonable. If your relationship with your immediate leader or team members has deteriorated beyond repair due to various circumstances, it may signal the need for a change. Personal conditioning and upbringing may influence your perception of job stability, potentially leading you to stay in roles longer than necessary.

My upbringing instilled in me an appreciation for stable employment which at times limited my perception of available opportunities and potential career paths. I often sought a sense of security within an organisation and remained in roles longer than necessary, even when I felt ready for a change. This tendency stemmed from my belief that job opportunities might be scarce elsewhere, as well as personal circumstances such as having partners or friends working nearby which influenced my decision to stay.

It's vital to challenge any limiting beliefs that may be keeping you stuck in a situation that no longer serves you. If after discussing concerns with your leaders and assessing feedback, you determine that the situation isn't conducive to personal or professional growth, it may be time to formulate an exit plan. Understand the policies and procedures of your organisation, recognising that adherence to these rules is typically non-negotiable. If you find yourself disengaged or lacking motivation to excel in your role, it could be a sign that your current environment is no longer conducive to your well-being.

I participated in a women's career development program aimed at helping women within the company identify their professional and personal aspirations while supporting them in reaching their full potential. The program involved seeking honest and specific feedback from various stakeholders on various aspects on my performance and behaviour through a survey. Topics included networking strategies, ways to enhance exposure and impact, managing work-life balance, and assessing communication styles ranging from passive to assertive to aggressive. Stakeholders were also asked about my effectiveness in saying no when necessary and how I communicated boundaries and priorities in the workplace.

I requested the general manager to complete the survey on my behalf, and he provided candid feedback. He noted areas where I could improve, such as my networking efforts, suggesting that I could demonstrate more active participation within the team rather than occasionally appearing as an observer. He also pointed out that he hadn't observed a strong emphasis on work over life. He said I could do my current role in my sleep and he questioned whether I wanted the additional stretch or was comfortable with my current role and did I want to do more?

Furthermore, he perceived me as passive and uncertain, advising that I should say "yes" more often and actively seek out opportunities to add value within my expertise and passions as I had more to offer. His words resonated deeply with me as I realised their accuracy. This feedback served as a pivotal moment, prompting me to acknowledge that I had reached the end of my journey with the company. This was not the way I normally behaved at work, nor the way I wanted to be.

Reflecting on my time there, I encountered numerous challenges, including ovarian cancer, difficult team dynamics, limited support from leadership, and insufficient recognition for my accomplishments. However, I took ownership of my role in these challenges, recognising I had run my course with this organisation and I was not performing at my optimum. I decided to move on, and resigned. It was one of the best decisions I've ever made.

WHAT GOOD LOOKS LIKE

Here are some examples of what good looks like when working in a collaborative organisation:

- Colleagues and leaders show genuine interest in you as a person. Simple acts like asking about your time off, remembering your plans and following up, checking in when you're sick encouraging you to rest, and expressing heartfelt concern during difficult times.

- When things go wrong, the focus is on learning from the incident rather than placing blame or causing humiliation. The goal is to understand the event and prevent it from happening again.

- There is camaraderie among colleagues and leaders. Enjoying each other's company, sharing laughs and making jokes are all part of the positive atmosphere.

- Team members help each other get the job done. The team is seen as a collective unit. If an individual is struggling to meet a deadline or simply needs a hand, other team members pitch in to help.

- The team comprises a mix of personalities. Team members recognise that everyone's differences are a strength, bringing diverse skills, experiences, and ideas that lead to better solutions and outcomes.

- Individuals are empowered to speak up, voice their opinions, and express concerns. Everyone is listened to and given the floor in meetings.

- You receive feedback on your performance in a genuine and honest manner. Whether it's verbal feedback or a thank-you email, it's done without fuss and is a natural part of the organisation's culture. The respect and appreciation are palpable.

- Consistency – you know what to expect and what you will get every time. People 'walk the talk'.

I've worked in these types of organisations – they exist.

CHAPTER 5

ASK FOR HELP WITHOUT FEELING LIKE YOU'RE LOSING FACE

5 ASK FOR HELP WITHOUT FEELING LIKE YOU'RE LOSING FACE

"One of the biggest defects in life is the inability to ask for help."
Robert Kiyosaki

Quiet Achievers can feel uncomfortable asking for help for the following reasons:

- They pride themselves on being self-sufficient and completing tasks independently - asking for help can feel like admitting a weakness or failure
- Asking for help can make them feel like they are not meeting their own expectations and the high standards they set for themselves
- It exposes them to scrutiny by drawing attention to themselves
- They worry that others may perceive them as less competent
- They worry about being seen as a burden if they perceive their colleagues and leader as busy
- If they lack confidence in their abilities, they fear asking for help will confirm their insecurities

"Growth and comfort do not coexist."
Ginni Rometty

Each time I asked for help I realised:

- It pushed me out of my comfort zone and I became more self-assured each time
- I came up with a better solution with the input of others than on my own
- It made my job easier and it was a way to highlight what I was working on
- No one thought I was incompetent

LEVERAGE THE EXPERTISE OF OTHERS

"Be resourceful."
Melissa Haggarty

A key principle is to remember you do not need to know everything. Your team, peers and work colleagues are your best resources. I used to waste time by procrastinating and feeling pressured to have all the solutions, fearing that others might perceive me as less intelligent if I didn't. Throughout my career as an industrial chemist, predominantly setting up and commissioning laboratories, I frequently had to navigate unfamiliar industries and processing plants. I had to quickly understand complex processes, analysis requirements, team structures, skill sets, required equipment and systems.

In these situations I realised the importance of leveraging the expertise of others. I became adept at identifying individuals who were more knowledgeable or experienced, whether within the organisation, the construction group or affiliated plants. This network of resources proved invaluable in navigating new territories and addressing challenges efficiently. I leveraged one-on-one interactions as this suited my preference as a Quiet Achiever.

Another critical aspect was establishing agreement on the scope of analytical services, given the stakeholders' interest in the laboratory's output. This involved targeting the appropriate audience, obtaining sign-offs, and documenting agreements. These steps not only facilitated the setup process but also provided clarity for future team members.

My motto is to simplify rather than complicate matters. I firmly believe in seeking assistance from those who have tackled similar tasks before. By tapping into existing knowledge and resources, you can achieve optimal results in the shortest possible time.

BE SPECIFIC

Instead of asking for help, frame it as asking for input or advice. This shifts the request from needing assistance to gaining a different perspective.

Focus on the task, not yourself. Discuss requiring input to ensure the success of the task. It is not because you are not capable.

When asking for input, clearly outline the type of input or advice you need, why you need it and any deadlines involved. Spend time before you ask for input, understanding your issue. Be prepared to articulate what you have done to solve it independently.

Highlight mutual benefit. Explain how the input will benefit both parties. Will it improve work efficiencies or the quality of work or outputs? Highlighting mutual benefits can make others more receptive to providing input.

NORMALISE ASKING FOR HELP

Everyone needs help at times. Asking for help is a natural part of teamwork and allows the team to feel invested in finding a solution.

Asking for help is not a sign of weakness or incompetence.

It demonstrates a commitment to achieving the best results.

Advocate for what you need to be successful in your role. Proactively define and request what you need and outline the potential consequences if these needs are not met.

"Don't be afraid to ask questions. Don't be afraid to ask for help when you need it. I do that every day. Asking for help isn't a sign of weakness, it's a sign of strength. It shows you have the courage to admit when you don't know something, and to learn something new."
Barack Obama

CHAPTER 6

MASTER YOUR EMOTIONS SO YOU FEEL LIKE YOU'RE IN CONTROL

6 MASTER YOUR EMOTIONS SO YOU FEEL LIKE YOU'RE IN CONTROL

"To master your emotions is not to suppress them. It is to process them with diligence and express them with intelligence."
Kam Taj

WHY WE NEED TO MASTER OUR EMOTIONS

Improved Decision–Making: Emotional control allows us to think clearly and evaluate situations objectively, rather than reacting impulsively, helping us make good decisions.

Greater Productivity: We focus better, and stay motivated when we master our emotions instead of the up-and-down roller coaster ride due to emotional fluctuations.

Better Communication and Enhanced Relationships: Mastering our emotions fosters more effective communication and promotes cooperation, improves conflict resolution by remaining calm and focusing on constructive dialogue and solutions.

Increased Resilience: Enables us to bounce back from adversity and maintain a positive outlook.

Better Health: Leads to better physical and mental health.

Professional Success: Those who manage their emotions well are often more successful in their careers, as they can navigate complex social dynamics and handle pressure effectively.

Be in Your Power: Gives us a sense of control over our lives, enabling us to respond to situations proactively rather than reactively, driven by our emotional reactions.

PURPOSE OF OUR EMOTIONS

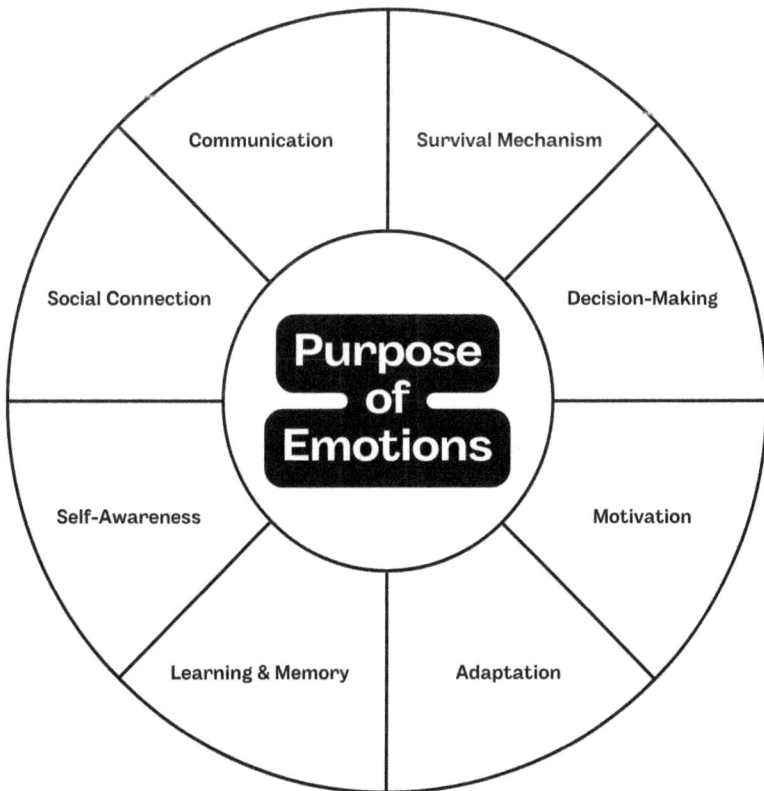

Survival Mechanism: Play a critical role in our survival by prompting quick responses to threats. For example, fear can trigger the fight-or-flight response preparing us to deal with danger.

Decision-Making: Emotions help us weigh options and make choices that align with our values and needs.

Motivation: Drives us to take action. Excitement drives us towards achieving our goals. Frustration can motivate us to change our circumstances.

Adaptation: Provide feedback on our experiences and helps us adjust our behaviours to changing environments and situations.

Learning and Memory: Emotional experiences are more memorable, helping us recall important information and lessons learned.

Self-Awareness: By providing insight into our inner self by helping us understand our desires, fears, strengths and weaknesses.

Social Connection: Shared emotional experiences demonstrating happiness and care creates a sense of community and belonging.

Communication: Emotions help us communicate our feelings to others, strengthening relationships.

UNDERSTAND YOUR EMOTIONS

Understanding what you are feeling is the first step to mastering your emotions. Be kind to yourself. Emotions are natural and it is necessary to feel and release them. As you become more aware of your emotions, your emotional regulation will increase. Mastering emotions is a continuous process. Be patient and persistent as learning to understand and regulate your emotions takes consistent effort.

Practice mindfulness so as to be present and become more aware of emotional shifts as they occur. This can be through meditation or as simple as taking a few deep breaths to become more focused. Write down your thoughts and feelings to help identify patterns and triggers. Be open and curious, keep digging until you uncover the root cause of the emotion you are feeling. Visualise yourself handling challenging emotional situations successfully. Regularly exercise, eat nourishing food for your body and get adequate sleep for emotional regulation.

Another way I get in tune with my emotions is by playing my medicine drum. In 2020, I created and birthed my own medicine drum. The vibration of the drum moves through my body, helping me relax and connect with my emotions instantly. The process of creating the drum was transformational. The animal which gifted me his hide had a temperamental energy, and things had to be done his way. The biggest lesson I learned during this process was to let go of control - you will receive exactly what you need.

To birth your own medicine drum, search for medicine drum-making workshops. Drum-making workshops by Alissa Meechan are featured in the Resources section at the back of the book.

NO FAILURE, ONLY FEEDBACK

View setbacks and challenges as opportunities for learning and improvement rather than as outright failures. Every experience, even if it doesn't go as planned, provides valuable feedback that can be used to adjust strategies, refine skills and ultimately achieve success in future endeavours.

Approach feedback with curiosity. If the feedback is unclear, embrace inquiring further. Ensure you fully comprehend the feedback provided by seeking clarification from the source, enabling you to extract valuable insights and grow from the experience.

When things don't go to plan, ask, "What do I need to learn?"

Journaling helps to discover the lessons you need to learn. Learn the lessons, or you will find similar experiences continue to show up until you do. Similar to getting hit with a feather, a book and eventually a bus.

"When the feather hits...
take notice and learn the lesson."
Melissa Haggarty

PERCEPTION IS PROJECTION - BE AT CAUSE

'Perception is projection' is a famous phrase from Carl Jung, a Swiss psychiatrist.

"Everything that irritates us about others can lead us to an understanding of ourselves."
Carl Jung

What we observe in others often highlights what we need to work on within ourselves. We all have traits we dislike about ourselves, and instead of acknowledging them we often project them onto others. The most negative emotions we feel about others often reflects issues within us. The world acts as a mirror, reflecting back our inner states. You cannot experience a trait in others that is not within you. Every situation, event or relationship mirrors aspects of yourself.

Each of us creates our own perception of reality. Our view of others and situations is shaped by our own internal representations influenced by our unconscious filters, including memories, decisions, values, beliefs and attitudes. If our reality is merely our perception, imagine the countless possibilities for how reality truly is. We tend to notice examples and situations in our reality that support our own thoughts and beliefs.

We all respond differently to the same situation. It is not the situation itself that bothers us, but our thoughts and beliefs about it. Be on the cause side, not the effect side. Choosing the cause side means recognising our perceptions and being open to exploring alternative perspectives. If we are courageous enough to acknowledge our own shortcomings, we can discover that our assumptions are not always accurate.

What Side Are You On?

Be At CAUSE!

RESULTS (CAUSE)	EXCUSES or REASONS (EFFECT)
Takes Responsibility	Blames
Decisive	Procrastinates
Proactive	Reactive
Action	Put up with
Opportunistic	Has to
Choice	No Choice
Powerful	Powerless
In control of own emotional states	Responds to other's emotional states
Initiative	Fatalistic
Makes things happen	Victim
Leader	Follower

Reference: Heslin, D. *NLP Practitioner Manual.* Debra Heslin Wellness, Inc. Link to NLP Practitioner Training https://www.debraheslinwellness.com/nlp-certification

What are the traits you dislike about the other person or situation?

What thoughts and emotions come up for you when you think about these traits?

Where have you seen these traits in yourself?

Journal as you unravel what comes up and keep going until you discover where these same traits show up in your life.

For example, if you feel that someone is not being entirely truthful with you, reflect on areas in your own life where you might not be fully honest. Are there parts of yourself that you're withholding from others? Are you being open and genuine in your interactions? What are you hiding from others? Why are you afraid of being seen and heard?

When I first embraced the idea that perception is projection, it felt like swallowing a bitter pill. If I didn't like how someone else behaved, why would I choose to behave the same way in my life? Yet the insights I gain about my inner self are always profound.

What we dislike in others reflects an internal filter, such as a thought, belief or attitude that has embedded itself in our unconscious mind. The results we experience provide feedback on how these filters are functioning. Our unconscious mind represses memories with unresolved negative emotions and brings them to our awareness for resolution. Essentially, your unconscious mind is presenting a repressed internal representation for acknowledgment.

Take back control by standing on the cause side and changing your projection. When you feel the projection arising, stop it, do the inner work to transform it, and reflect using filters that create the reality you desire.

HANDLING CONFLICT

Stick to the facts and keep emotions out of it. If necessary, release emotions through writing or other outlets before addressing the issue. When faced with a challenging team member, I sought assistance from a friend who listened as I described the situation. He asked clarifying questions to keep me focused specifically on the unsatisfactory performance and stopped me when I veered into emotions and unnecessary storytelling. This process greatly aided me in gaining clarity on the issue.

Remember, conflicts are mostly not personal. People operate from their own filters based on their perspectives and biases. Understand that each person's reality is shaped by their unique perceptions. The map is not the territory. Their reality is not your reality. However, for each individual, their perception is the reality to them.

The concept of being 'not the right fit for the job' exists. The first step is to accept this concept. There is a point where you have to stop bending over backwards to work with certain individuals. Depending on how effectively the individuals manage their emotions, accepting this and moving forward can be a challenging process.

PATTERN INTERRUPT

Do you ever find yourself in an unresourceful state? For example, when you become frustrated or angry, you might 'see red' and fixate on your anger. This mindset does not help you to move past your anger into a resourceful state.

A pattern interrupt is a technique to shift your emotional state by doing something unexpected or unusual - move your body, shout, do a silly dance, or speak in a funny voice. Instead of focusing on the negative emotion, engage in an activity that demands your attention. Changing your physical state changes how you feel.

Consider driving and how easily other drivers can frustrate you. My Dad regularly called other drivers 'turkeys'. When I get frustrated with other drivers, I call them 'turkeys' too; it always makes me giggle and reminds me of Dad – a great way to break the pattern of frustration.

I use walking as a pattern interrupt. At one organisation, I had a five-minute walk between the operations building and the laboratory. If I left a meeting frustrated, I would spend those five minutes calming down and identifying what had upset me.

I've also taken team members for walks around the site when they've been frustrated and angry. Typically, I say very little while they vent their feelings. By the end of the walk, once they've calmed down, I ask what actions need to be taken. Since they've returned to a resourceful state, they can access the answers they need.

GET A COACH

"I absolutely believe that people, unless coached, never reach their maximum capabilities."
Bob Nardelli

Throughout my career in various industries, I've had different mentors and never a personal coach. I did participate in numerous leadership and development programs within the industry. Now, as the owner of my own coaching business, I have my own coach, and it's been a transformative decision. I chose my coach because I identified she could get me to where I wanted to be, in the quickest way possible.

A coach helps you move from A to B, pain to pleasure. They assist you in overcoming obstacles and moving forward with momentum. They help you get clear on your action steps and understand your thought patterns and behaviours. Having a coach is essential for success in your professional and personal life.

Coaching can help improve all areas of your life, including both work and personal matters. For example, when someone expresses anger at work, it often signals deeper issues that affect all aspects of their life – they may be angry at home and in their relationships too. Many of us don't realise how our thoughts, beliefs and behaviours can limit us and shape our experiences and interactions. While you're responsible for doing the work, a coach holds you accountable, helping you move forward and succeed. Why remain trapped in your self-imposed limitations?

CHAPTER 7

LOOK GOOD IN YOUR LEADER'S EYES

7 LOOK GOOD IN YOUR LEADER'S EYES

Your leader is instrumental in promoting you, the Quiet Achiever, and helping you thrive and gain the recognition you deserve.

It is important for a Quiet Achiever to look good in their leader's eyes because:

- It ensures your skills and contributions are noticed and valued leading to acknowledgement in meetings or reports
- Being recognised leads to promotions, new responsibilities and career development
- Leaders can create or offer platforms for you to share your ideas including presentations and team collaborations
- Leaders often allocate resources based on perceived value and being recognised leads to better support for projects and performing role responsibilities

UNDERSTAND WHAT YOUR LEADER VALUES

What are the priorities, expectations and ways of working that your leader values?

Do they value direct or detailed communication?
Do they value flexibility, reliability or initiative?
Do they value teamwork or independent work?
How do they want to be informed of the status of your tasks?

Understanding your leader's values helps you tailor your work to meet expectations and improve your overall performance.

TAILOR YOUR COMMUNICATION TO SUIT YOUR LEADER'S PREFERENCES AND STYLE

Quiet Achievers, once they understand what is required of them, generally prefer to be left to their own devices to delve into their work and fulfil responsibilities. While their independent approach ensures tasks are completed, it may pose challenges if their contributions are integral to broader team objectives and go unnoticed upon completion.

Quiet Achievers must ascertain the level of communication their leaders expect from them.

How frequently does your leader expect updates on your work or the team's progress?

Consider the reporting process: Is it formal or informal? Weekly, monthly, quarterly? Are there pre-start meetings or team planning meetings? Is there an optimal day for reporting that accommodates other reporting obligations?

Establish a formal reporting process if none exists, which will help document your activities for performance reviews.

The key is to discover what makes your leader feel assured that you have your workload under control. When there's confidence in the Quiet Achiever's capabilities, the leader will grant them autonomy to complete their work which aligns well with the Quiet Achiever's preferences.

In initial discussions with a new leader, I emphasise my preferred working style and the importance I place on autonomy. I seek clarification on reporting expectations and convey to my leader that if I seek their presence or request their time, it's because I genuinely require their input.

Quiet Achievers invest time to find the right solution. They must guard against overanalysing, going round and round in circles and procrastination before arriving at a decision. If you're still refining a task without a definitive solution, maintain communication about your progress. Avoid staying silent due to uncertainty: instead, convey where you are at. Transparent communication is preferable to silence when unsure.

Take caution if you are a female updating a male counterpart on your progress, as men and women often approach decision-making differently. Women typically prefer to explore various solutions, gather data, and communicate concerns. In contrast, men tend to run straight to the finish line with a plan of action. When men hear questions and concerns from a woman, they may interpret it as a request for a plan of action or, worse, perceive the woman as incompetent. This can lead to frustration for the woman, who may feel the man is rushing to solve the problem without considering all relevant data and concerns.

I found myself in this exact situation when tasked with achieving ISO 9001 for a site. Whilst discussing the resources I needed for success with the general manager, he bluntly remarked, "I thought with your quality background, you were the right person for the job". Feeling taken aback, I swiftly concluded the discussion and left. Upon reflection, I realised that I had delved into various options and concerns, while all he sought was information on what resources I required so he could say yes or no. Returning to him, I expressed how his comment made me feel like a 'dimwit' and my perception of how the conversation had gone wrong. Despite the hiccup, I still secured the necessary resources for the project.

ALWAYS SEEK CLARITY

Clarity is essential to ensure you are working on the right tasks at the right time. As a Quiet Achiever, it may seem easier to stay silent and avoid asking questions. However, this approach can come back to bite you. There is nothing more frustrating for a Quiet Achiever than realising they've been pursuing the wrong path for some time, wasting effort on unnecessary tasks. If a question arises about your work, don't hesitate to address it promptly.

Even if it feels uncomfortable, taking action to seek clarity has two potential outcomes. Firstly, you may confirm you are on the right track, providing reassurance and allowing you to proceed confidently. Alternatively, you might discover that you've veered off course, enabling you to correct your path promptly and focus on what's truly necessary.

WORK WITH EASE

Approach everything with a sense of ease, from your interactions, task assignments to receiving work, progress updates and status reports. This also includes suggestions, participation and adapting to new ideas and tasks. Ensure you are not creating obstacles for yourself. Stay mindful that your own barriers aren't hindering progress or blocking your path forward.

Identifying your own barriers requires self-awareness and honest reflection. Here are some steps to help you identify your own barriers:

- Journal – write about your thoughts, behaviours and emotions
- Identify patterns in your behaviour that lead to negative outcomes or stagnation. Look for habits that consistently result in frustration or setbacks

- Acknowledge when you fall into unproductive patterns and commit to making changes
- Ask yourself if your beliefs are truly serving you or limiting your potential
- Practice mindfulness or meditate to tune in to your thoughts and emotions in the moment
- Embrace the discomfort and be willing to face uncomfortable truths about yourself
- Focus on what you want and take actionable steps towards improvement

Given the significant amount of time spent at work, it's vital to streamline your experience at work and make it as easy as possible. Additionally, making your leader's job and overall experience at work smoother is advantageous for both the business and your leader.

In my experience, my most valued team members were those who consistently made my job easy.

DIVERSIFY

I faced a challenge where I felt restricted by the confines of working solely within the laboratory due to the specificity of the role. Recognising the need to broaden my skills, I sought opportunities to diversify. I aimed to gain insights into various levels of management and understand how the business operated. So, I pursued a secondment in human resources, viewing it as a chance to expand my knowledge. Ultimately I was offered a permanent position within the human resources team.

There are diverse ways to achieve this, such as traineeships, apprenticeships or accepting different projects within your current role. Additionally, engaging in team activities like barbecues or fundraising events can foster connections with colleagues across departments. While your main stakeholders are crucial, don't overlook opportunities to interact with others within your workplace, for example through project focus groups.

It's essential to be strategic. I've observed individuals who, out of discontent, grasped at any opportunity that came their way, impacting their credibility. Therefore, it's crucial to discern what you genuinely want and pursue it strategically. With my change into human resources, I had a specific goal in mind and pursued it persistently.

FOSTER RESPECT

Certain leadership behaviours garner respect from team members. Behaviours include clearly communicating expectations, acknowledging individual contributions, trusting their decisions, treating everyone equitably, acting with honesty and transparency, honouring their commitments, being open to feedback and demonstrating a commitment to excellence. Respect is one of my top five values at work, and I am happiest when it is mutual.

Acknowledge and express gratitude for the work your leader does. Offer a simple "thank you" to show appreciation. Demonstrate genuine interest in their activities, even if they don't directly involve you.

Quiet Achievers may find it difficult to show respect to their leader in certain situations.

Some examples of these situations are:

- If their efforts and achievements are overshadowed by the Loud Achievers who seek visibility and their contributions go unnoticed
- When a leader assumes the Quiet Achiever is remaining quiet because they have nothing to contribute versus realising the Quiet Achiever prefers to reflect on relevant information before speaking up and expressing their opinion
- When organisations celebrate the achievements of Loud Achievers and overlook the value added by Quiet Achievers
- If Quiet Achievers are pushed to behave in a manner that is not authentic, for example, be forced to act louder than desired to be recognised

Inevitably, there will be moments when your leader annoys you. There will be times when you question their choices, decisions and motivations. My definition of respect means recognising that your leader is fulfilling their role to the best of their ability, based on what they know. Sometimes, your leader makes decisions and you may not be privy to all the information that led to those decisions. As humans, we all base our decisions on available information using our own unique decision-making strategies. So, never jump to conclusions that your leader is incompetent. Making decisions always involves considering various factors. If there are aspects you don't understand about certain tasks, goals or how the business reached certain decisions, don't hesitate to ask questions to gain clarity. And remember, if you disagree or believe there's a better approach, share your feedback. However, ultimately, if your feedback doesn't lead to further changes, it's important to accept the decision and get on with the job. Continuing to carry the annoyance will impact you far more than it will impact your leader.

If your leader consistently demonstrates behaviours that fail to cultivate respect, it's crucial to assess the benefit of remaining in the same role and potentially within the organisation, particularly if the lack of respect is a cultural issue. If this is where you are now, assuming you started reading the book at the beginning, you will have read my suggestions in the section 'When It Stops Working – Move On' in the chapter titled 'Shine Bright And Not Burn Out'.

CREATE YOUR WORK ENVIRONMENT

Our environment affects our performance in various ways.

Our physical environment plays a significant role. Factors such as an uncomfortable chair, uncomfortable working temperature or a cluttered space can cause discomfort and fatigue, reducing productivity. A clutter-free, organised, quiet, aesthetically pleasing environment promotes focus and efficiency. Additionally, access to the right tools and technology is crucial for enabling efficiency and problem-solving.

Our social environment, the quality of relationships and workplace culture also impacts performance. Positive interactions, a collaborative atmosphere and a supportive environment make the workplace more enjoyable and conducive to productivity.

Let's focus on the social environment aspect. While you can't control other people's actions and behaviours, you can control how you behave and act toward others.

The Law of Attraction suggests that like attracts like. This is why we need to focus on and believe in what we want instead of what we don't. In the workplace, individuals with similar work ethics, values and attitudes will naturally work better together.

To contribute to a supportive work environment and affirm the value of working together, consider actions such as:

- Punctuality and preparation for meetings
- Timely provision of requested information
- Openly praising your leader and peers when they do a good job
- Solving problems
- Offering constructive feedback, highlighting areas for improvement with appropriate language
- Celebrating wins – do this at the start of your weekly meeting
- Say "thank you" to show appreciation

ADDRESS ISSUES

"Nip it in the bud."
Sir Boyle Roche

Address issues rather than letting them stew. We all have different ways of responding when something feels off; some of us take longer to process why we feel that way, while others may respond immediately, either diplomatically or defensively. However, avoiding conflict or staying quiet can lead to missed opportunities for learning and growth.

If you're naturally quiet and prefer to avoid conflict, you might feel hesitant to speak up due to various reasons: feeling like you have nothing valuable to share, fearing repercussions, worrying about being disliked, or simply being a people-pleaser. But by keeping quiet, you allow negative emotions to linger inside your body and potentially distort your perception of the situation.

It's important to recognise that your perception or assumptions about an event may not always be accurate. Sometimes, you may be completely off the mark, other times you may be partially correct. Therefore, it's essential to address the issue rather than internalising it.

Personally, I tend to take longer to realise when something feels off for me and to identify what's bothering me. In such situations, it's crucial to find the courage to speak up or take action. In some situations it's okay to revisit the issue later and express your feelings, perhaps by asking questions to gain clarity. You may find that your perceptions were incorrect and there's no need to continue feeling the negative emotion.

Additionally, be mindful not to internalise the thoughts and opinions of others, as this can also contribute to unnecessary stress and discomfort. Ultimately, addressing issues and expressing your feelings constructively is essential for personal growth and maintaining healthy relationships.

Establish clear expectations and boundaries. Understand what boundaries are and their significance. A boundary is essentially a delineation that defines what is acceptable and unacceptable to you, what you will tolerate and what you won't, how you prefer to operate, and your expectations for interactions with others. It's a tool for asserting your personal power and maintaining clarity about your limits.

Examples of boundaries in the workplace:

- I am available for work from 8am to 6pm
- I will respond to emails and messages within twenty-four hours during workdays
- I prefer to schedule meetings between 11am and 2pm to ensure I have uninterrupted time for focused work

- For urgent matters, please call me. For non-urgent issues, email is preferred.
- Please do not interrupt me unless urgent when I have my 'Do Not Disturb' sign on
- I prefer to address conflicts in private and calmly discuss solutions
- Meetings must start and end on time. If additional time is needed, let's schedule a follow-up.
- I prefer to keep my personal life separate from work. Please respect my privacy.

When others' behaviour violates your boundaries, it's crucial to take action and speak up. By firmly standing in your own power, you'll likely encounter fewer instances of boundary violations, though occasional tests are inevitable. When faced with such tests, enforce your boundaries and communicate clearly to those around you when they cross the line.

Top tips for speaking up when your boundaries are crossed:

- Nip it in the bud
- Remove the emotions. Get clear on the boundary that was crossed and how it affects you.
- Be specific. Example – "When meetings run over the scheduled time, it impacts my commitments following the meeting. I feel frustrated when I am late for my next commitment".
- Clearly state what change you desire moving forward. Example – "I would appreciate it if we can respect meeting start and finish times and schedule a follow-up meeting if we need more than the allotted time".
- Give the person the benefit of the doubt and listen to their perspective. They may not realise they crossed your boundary.

- Always make a note of the conversation and any agreements made, even when you think it isn't that serious. The issue may persist and become more serious or a repeat violation.

- Seek support if you need. Perhaps from a leader, HR or a trusted person.

One of the presuppositions of NLP is: Everyone is doing the best they can with the resources they have available. Behaviour is geared for adaptation and present behaviour is the best choice available. Every behaviour is motivated by a positive intent.

Reference: Heslin, D. *NLP Practitioner Manual.* Debra Heslin Wellness, Inc. Link to NLP Practitioner Training https://www.debraheslinwellness.com/nlp-certification

This has helped me understand why we behave the way we do and to express when others' behaviour towards me is not acceptable based on my boundaries.

NAVIGATE OFFICE POLITICS

As a Quiet Achiever, I have never been one to engage in office politics. Engaging in office politics drains my energy and distracts me from my primary focus of getting my work done. I value honesty, fairness and integrity and I've found these values can be compromised by office politics leading to manipulation and dishonesty. Whilst I don't engage in office politics, I have learned how to navigate them.

- I am aware of the main players in office politics and make sure I remain neutral and do not engage in being part of the main group

- I ensure my communication is clear, concise and respectful

- I stay true to my values and ethics, even if I'm pushed to waver

- I let my work speak for itself by consistently delivering quality results
- I focus on building relationships with colleagues and leaders to foster trust and support

TRAIN OTHERS TO TAKE YOUR JOB

It's essential to train others to take on your responsibilities. Throughout my career, I've encountered individuals who cling tightly to their roles and work, projecting an aura of protectiveness stemming from a fear of being replaceable. I approach this differently; I embrace the idea of being replaceable because it signifies growth and the acquisition of new skills that can be applied elsewhere or in other roles. This mindset allows for continual learning and development.

One tangible benefit of training others to handle your tasks is evident when you go on holidays. Having someone you've already trained to fill in for you ensures continuity in your absence, which benefits you and your leader. Facilitating this arrangement creates appreciation and support with your leader. Additionally, your leader may appreciate your input on potential candidates to fill your role or have their own plans for the team's succession.

Regardless of how the arrangement is structured, whether it's identifying someone to cover during your absence or grooming a successor, it's crucial to have these discussions with your leader. Embrace the opportunity to train others in your work; it not only benefits the organisation but also opens up new avenues for personal growth and advancement for yourself.

CHAPTER 8

THE SECRETS TO BEING NOTICED IN PERFORMANCE REVIEWS

8 THE SECRETS TO BEING NOTICED IN PERFORMANCE REVIEWS

A performance review is a periodic formal assessment in which an employee's job performance and overall contribution to the organisation are evaluated. Formal performance reviews can be conducted monthly, quarterly or annually.

They include:

- Reviewing how well the employee has performed their duties and responsibilities over a defined period, generally related to their Role/Position Description
- Providing feedback on strengths and areas for improvement
- Reviewing how well the employee has completed set goals and updating future goals to reflect any change in the organisation's goals
- Developing new goals to develop in the areas requiring improvement
- Reviewing compensation in the form of salary adjustments or bonuses linked to performance
- Discussing opportunities for professional development, training and promotions
- Discussing any concerns about the job and clarify expectations
- Providing feedback on your leader's performance
- Documenting the review as a record of progress

In short, a performance review helps an employee understand:

- What they're doing right
- Where they need to improve
- How their work contributes to the organisation's business plan, what has changed and what updates are required

A performance review is typically conducted between the employee and their immediate leader, aligning well with the Quiet Achiever's preference for private acknowledgment. The main challenge for Quiet Achievers is the discomfort they feel when they need to shine the spotlight on their work, making it visible. When things feel uncomfortable, the easiest way to make it more comfortable is implement a system and follow the system. Since Quiet Achievers are motivated by the satisfaction of their work and results, implement a system that helps you record your achievements and results. It will shift it to be like completing another task, versus shining the spotlight on your work.

If your organisation conducts regular performance reviews, they will have a performance review process documented and in place. The first step in setting yourself up for a successful performance review is to understand how the performance review process works and what is expected of you. Find the documentation detailing the performance review process with associated templates to use.

The following sections will explain how to design your performance recording system and what you need to know about the organisation's performance review process.

Consider informal ways to discuss your progress if your organisation doesn't conduct formal performance reviews. Schedule a regular check-in with your leader to discuss the status of your work, ask for feedback, identify areas where you need training and development and discuss any concerns. Ask for feedback from colleagues, stakeholders and customers to get a wider view of how others perceive your performance.

ALIGN WORK PLAN WITH ORGANISATIONAL GOALS

Organisations typically conduct a business planning exercise each year, outlining the organisations' vision, strategy, objectives, goals and deliverables including stakeholder and customer requirements.

Align your yearly deliverables and goals with your team's deliverables and the overarching business plan and strategy. This helps you understand how your role fits in the organisation. Below is a simple diagram to demonstrate how you achieve alignment.

For example, an aligned goal looks like:
1. The organisation sets goal 1.1.
2. Your Leader sets goal 1.1 which is specifically what your Leader is going to do to help the organisation achieve their goal 1.1.
3. You set goal 1.1 which is specifically what you are going to do to help your Leader achieve their goal 1.1 and in turn the organisation achieve their goal 1.1.

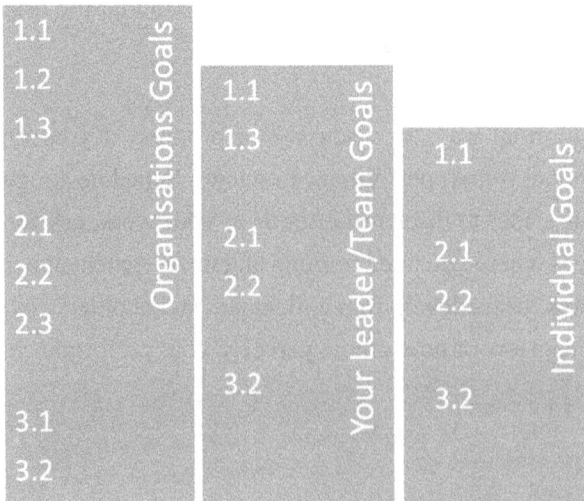

EXAMPLE

Organisational Goal	Team Goals	Individual Goals
2.2 Complete plant operation and test program as identified in project plan	2.2a Ensure all heat mass balance runs are complete by 30 June 2.2b Crushing and screening completed with first product available by 30 May	2.2a External sample analysis and procedures in place to support heat mass balance runs by 31 March 2.2b Commission all analysers and approve documentation including procedures and training competencies and train personnel by 30 April

Goals should be written SMART. A SMART goal defines clear and actionable objectives.

S   Specific
M   Measurable
A   Achievable
R   Relevant
T   Time-bound

SMART goals give clarity between leaders and employees on specific requirements and the criteria for success. When goals are well-defined it becomes easier to confirm their completion.

YOUR PERFORMANCE RECORDING SYSTEM

Why do you need your own system for recording your achievements and results?

- It can be challenging to remember your achievements from a week ago, let alone over an entire year for an annual performance review
- Documenting your achievements builds self-belief as you reflect on your progress and successes and highlights your strengths and areas for improvement
- Keeping a record and view of your routine, ad-hoc and additional tasks helps you stay organised and alerts you early if any tasks are getting off track
- Tracking the status of your tasks prepares you for both planned and unplanned conversations with your leader about your work's progress, allowing for more productive and informed conversations
- Keeping a detailed record ensures you can accurately present your achievements, making your performance review more comprehensive, demonstrating your growth over time

Keep your performance recording system simple. For me, this is using an Excel spreadsheet. Use any software that you are familiar with. Organise this information in a format that can be easily shared.

Learn how your performance rating is scored. Is it percentage-based across different areas? Is it based on daily duties, goal completion and or safety performance? Understand the scoring criteria and structure your performance recording system accordingly.

As a minimum, if your performance is evaluated across different areas, set up your performance tracking system to reflect those areas.

Schedule regular updates to your performance tracking system in your calendar, either weekly or monthly. If you have regular reporting commitments to your leader, align your updates with this frequency since you will already be focused on the status of your work. Record the detail of your achievements, your successes and things you would do differently next time.

If you realise that you are not going to meet a goal, or a goal has become redundant, address it with your leader promptly and update your objectives to reflect the new agreement. Do not wait until the annual performance review to discuss any challenges.

Ensure there is a section to record additional tasks you have completed. Think of it as gathering factual data. This helps Quiet Achievers recognise where they are going above and beyond. These extra activities, beyond your routine job and set goals, contribute to a higher performance rating and can result in extra dollars in your pocket, a way better outcome than not getting recognised for your efforts.

PREPARE FOR YOUR PERFORMANCE REVIEW DISCUSSION

Typically, leaders will conduct a formal face-to-face meeting with their team members to discuss their performance over the year. Performance reviews are a two-way conversation. There should be no surprises for either the leader or the team member, except in the case of a recent issue. Gather your notes and evidence of targets met and additional projects or tasks. Use language stating targets met, completed projects, completed goals, safely and on time, and positive feedback from customers and stakeholders. This reinforces your value to the organisation. Analyse the reasons behind any incomplete tasks so you can explain the reasons for missing the set targets.

Consider your strengths and areas for improvement. Is there any training or personal development you need? Link this to addressing your areas for improvement. Communicate your career goals and aspirations so that any necessary steps can be discussed and added to your plan.

I take a printed copy of my Excel spreadsheet to my performance review. If your organisation requires you to complete a self-review before the face-to-face meeting, take a printed copy of your submitted review notes with you.

Since you have already recorded your achievements, discussing them is easy. It's just another step in the review process.

Be prepared to provide your leader with feedback on their performance noting where they have supported you well and where they could improve.

Maintain a positive attitude and express enjoyment of specific tasks or activities. Be the most energetic person in the room as your enthusiasm can influence others. Use what you have learned about building rapport from the 'Get Recognised Without Feeling Like A Show Off' chapter to positively influence your leader's emotions and responsiveness.

At times we are uncertain about feedback we receive from our leader. How to deal with this has been covered in the section 'No Failure, Only Feedback' in the chapter 'Master Your Emotions So You Feel Like You're In Control'.

KEY PERFORMANCE REVIEW DISCUSSION POINTS

- Achieved targets, emphasising the how (safely, on time)
- Additional completed activities (over and above set targets or role expectations)
- How you added value to the organisation, stakeholders and customers
- Reasons for missing set targets
- Your strengths and areas for improvement
- Training or personal development needed to address areas for improvement
- Your career goals and aspirations
- Feedback on your leader's performance

CHAPTER 9

PLAY TO YOUR STRENGTHS AND DISCOVER HOW TO SAY NO

9 PLAY TO YOUR STRENGTHS AND DISCOVER HOW TO SAY NO

Key strengths Quiet Achievers possess include:

- Problem-solving skills as they approach tasks methodically
- Attention to detail ensuring accuracy and quality in their work
- Persistence and patience in working through challenges until resolution
- Consistently delivering on their commitments
- Working autonomously and managing their work with minimal supervision
- Resilience, able to navigate change and uncertainty calmly

PLAN, PRIORITISE, AND ADAPT

"The key is not to prioritise what's on your schedule, but to schedule your priorities."
Stephen Covey

Plan, prioritise, and adapt accordingly. Quiet Achievers typically embrace the dynamic nature of shifting priorities in our ever-changing world. Recognise that we all have the same twenty-four hours each day and understand the time required for various activities.

"Poor planning on your part does not necessitate an emergency on mine."
Bob Carter

This quote was a favourite of one of my leaders. This quote serves to remind us it is not reasonable for our lack of preparation to impose urgency or crisis upon others. It encourages planning and responsibility for taking action. Anticipate obstacles and plan accordingly.

Throw out the concept of work-life balance. The word 'balance' suggests that it requires meticulous effort and precision – like balancing a spinning ball on your finger. The balance point is so delicate, that aiming to maintain balance consistently sets us up for inevitable failure, which is incredibly exhausting. Instead, **focus on prioritising**. To succeed, you will need to focus more on certain tasks or goals to get them done, letting others move down the list of priorities. Inherently, this means your to-do list will always be out of balance.

"Success is simple. Do what's right, the right way at the right time."
Arnold H. Glasow

Stay flexible. Flexibility requires the ability to adapt, pivot, rebound, negotiate and navigate through change. How adeptly we handle such situations often hinges on how well we are managing our lives. If you start to feel overwhelmed, pause and address the cause. You are responsible for you and know best how to take care of yourself.

Understand your personality type and your preferences, and choose goals that will enable you to highlight your strengths. I offer personality profiling as part of my coaching package. Personality profiles describe how people are likely to behave, they are not definitive guidelines. They outline our strengths and weaknesses and offer suggestions for personal growth. Personality is one aspect of many – our actions are influenced by our environment, experiences, goals, beliefs and values.

Streamline meetings to create uninterrupted work time. Ensure your energy is focused on your number one priority. Keep the focus on the primary purpose of the business, avoiding unnecessary distractions.

FOLLOW THE SYSTEM

Utilise processes and systems. Learn to use them effectively and efficiently and promptly address any issues or glitches. This allows Quiet Achievers to identify improvements and contribute suggestions for enhancements. Your work will go smoother if you follow established processes and systems rather than working around them. Adhering to procedures demonstrates reliability and consistency, allowing you to focus on tasks and build trust reinforcing your dependability.

The structure provided by systems helps Quiet Achievers feel confident in their roles, knowing what is expected of them. By following systems they can more easily collaborate with others, as everyone is on the same page regarding expectations and workflows.

LEARN HOW TO SAY NO

Quiet Achievers can easily become overwhelmed by their workload after saying yes to extra tasks since they are reliable in delivering on their commitments. Know your capacity. Be aware of your workload and be realistic about how long it takes to complete tasks. Identify your top priorities and deadlines to see which tasks can be deferred to accommodate new ones.

Watch the boundaries and expectations you set. For example, when I was commissioning a laboratory, I routinely worked extra hours each day. Once the laboratory was operational, I returned to normal working hours, but colleagues questioned if I was sick because they hadn't seen me as much. It took a few months for the comments to stop and normal hours to be accepted and I remained calm as I patiently set my new boundaries.

Protect your time blocks in your ideal week. Schedule dedicated time for your most important tasks, making it easier to say no to interruptions or additional tasks. Before saying yes, evaluate if the request aligns with your goals and strengths.

Say, "I don't have the capacity to commit to this right now, but I can help with ...." or suggest another person, a later time, or negotiate which of your existing tasks can be deferred to accommodate the new request.

Saying "no" is like managing a bookshelf. Imagine your time and energy as the space available on your bookshelf. Each book represents a task, commitment or responsibility. When your bookshelf is full, adding a new book requires you to remove an existing one. Similarly, when your schedule is packed, taking on new commitments means you must let go of some current ones to make room.

Just as a well-organised bookshelf reflects careful selection of books that truly matter to you, saying "no" ensures you prioritise what is most important. This allows you to focus on what you need to and prevents your shelf from becoming overcrowded and chaotic.

I have used the bookshelf analogy when saying no to family and friends. It allows me to feel comfortable with saying no because I'm simply putting them on hold. Their 'book' is still on my shelf, it just has to wait for now. This analogy helps me discuss with them what I need to focus on and lets them know when I'll return to their 'book' on my shelf.

Saying no is essential for maintaining your well-being and productivity when you do not have the capacity for additional tasks. Overcommitting can lead to burnout and decreased performance.

"Either you run the day, or the day runs you."
Jim Rohn

AUTHOR'S FINAL WORD

There is no such thing as final......our journey continues......always learning and growing.

"The capacity to learn is a gift; the ability to learn is a skill; the willingness to learn is a choice."
Brian Herbert

I want you to know - I see you, I hear you, I applaud you.

Embrace your unique strengths as a Quiet Achiever. Remember, standing out doesn't require changing who you are but rather leveraging your inherent qualities to make an impact.

The journey of a Quiet Achiever is not about conforming to the loudness of the world but about finding and amplifying your own voice in a way that is authentic to you. It's about recognising that your quiet nature is not a limitation but a powerful asset that brings depth, thoughtfulness, and a unique perspective to any situation.

As you move forward, keep in mind the strategies and insights shared in this book. Use them as tools to navigate your path with confidence, whether in your professional life, personal relationships or any other area where you wish to make an impact.

Celebrate your successes, no matter how small they may seem, and continue to grow and evolve as a person who is seen and heard in their own distinctive way. The world needs Quiet Achievers like you—those who lead with quiet strength, create meaningful change and inspire others through their authentic presence.

Thank you for embarking on this journey with me. May you always find the courage to stand out and the wisdom to know that your quiet power is invaluable.

With gratitude,

Melissa Haggarty

ABOUT THE AUTHOR
Author, Coach, Speaker, Animal Communicator

Hailing from central Queensland, Australia, Melissa's journey is nothing short of intriguing. An international best-selling author, certified master coach, and animal communicator, she's on a mission to help individuals, business owners and leaders to create their desired futures.

Melissa's life story unfolds with a twist. She started her career as an industrial chemist which led her through various industries and processing plants, grounding her in the world of industrial chemistry. Melissa has worked in liquefied natural gas (LNG), oil refining, alumina refining, ammonium nitrate processing and magnesium refining.

Today she's the proud owner of Integrated Soul, where she specialises in coaching and animal communication. Melissa helps her clients achieve the changes they desire. Within her coaching toolkit, she utilises neuro-linguistic programming (NLP), timeline therapy, hypnosis and soul and energy medicine techniques. Drawing from over two decades of industry experience, she offers leadership and personal organisation wisdom with a twist of soulful insight.

Beyond her professional accolades, Melissa is a member of the SMJ Coaching Institute, the American Board of Hypnotherapy, the American Board of Neuro-Linguistic Programming and the International Institute for Complementary Therapists.

When she's not delving into the depths of the soul, Melissa enjoys the vibrational beats of rock concerts balanced with the simplicity of camping.

Her travels, both in Australia and overseas, have a unique twist – she's on a quest to discover historical bridges. Melissa has visited the United States, China, Hong Kong, Singapore, Malaysia, Egypt, South Africa, Tanzania, Zimbabwe, Botswana, Fiji, New Caledonia and Vanuatu.

Melissa Haggarty is the author of *Quiet Achievers – How to be seen and heard so you stand out.* And her home? It's a peaceful haven overlooking Gladstone Harbour in central Queensland.

Melissa's life is a blend of science, soul, and adventure, a journey filled with delightful surprises. She has evolved from an industrial lab-rat into a bullshit buster, soul-driven and dream-life shaper.

RECOMMENDED RESOURCES

UNLOCK YOUR POTENTIAL

Celebrate transformation with Melissa, a seasoned professional in coaching and leadership. Melissa will guide you on this transformative journey. Her coaching services are dedicated to helping you find the right path, initiate action, and shape your dream life.

ARE YOU ON THE RIGHT PATH?

ARE YOU ON A JOURNEY THAT TRULY BELONGS TO YOU?

ARE YOU READY TO CREATE THE LIFE YOU DESIRE?

AT A GLANCE

- Personalised Coaching
- Breakthrough Strategies
- Goal Oriented Action Plans

In January 2021, a pivotal moment unfolded in Melissa's life. She was resigning from her twenty-year-long career as an Industrial Chemist. Melissa embraced the liberation from the confines of a large corporation and the rigid Monday-to-Friday routine. Purchasing a bongo van marked the beginning of her journey of self-discovery, a voyage that unfolded over twelve transformative months.

Melissa is precisely where she needs to be now, to assist people worldwide. As a coach, she empowers you to delve inward, gain clarity on your next steps and ultimately move forward.

BOOK AN INSIGHT CALL TODAY

TO DISCUSS HOW MELISSA CAN HELP YOU

"A coach is someone who tells you what you don't want to hear, who has you see what you don't want to see, so you can be who you have always known you could be." -Tom Landry

Integrated
S O U L

connect@integratedsoul.com.au
www.integratedsoul.com.au

WORKSHOPS

Does your team require assistance in:

- ✓ Managing stress and anxiety
- ✓ Enhancing customer service
- ✓ Unlocking peak performance
- ✓ Achieving business objectives
- ✓ Maximising productivity
- ✓ Boosting confidence
- ✓ Improving leadership

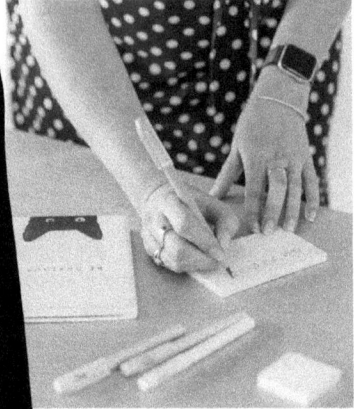

WHEN YOUR TEAM WORKS WITH MELISSA IN A GROUP WORKSHOP, YOU AND YOUR TEAM WILL CONQUER CHALLENGES, AND IDENTIFY THE OBSTACLES PREVENTING EACH INDIVIDUAL FROM ACHIEVING YOUR TEAM OBJECTIVES. THIS WILL TRANSFORM YOUR TEAM AND ALLOW YOUR TEAM TO ATTAIN YOUR DESIRED OUTCOMES.

CONTACT MELISSA TO DISCUSS NOW

Integrated
SOUL

connect@integratedsoul.com.au
www.integratedsoul.com.au

Alissa Meechan - Self-Mastery Initiator

W: www.alissameechan.com
E: hello@alissameechan.com
P: 0419 175 427

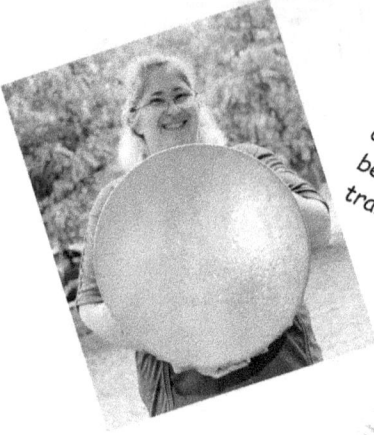

Whether you choose to make a Medicine Drum for your own personal healing or offer its magic to heal others, this drum making experience can be inspiring, powerful and transformational.

Who is Alissa Meechan

An energy feeler,
A Medicine Drumming Healer
And a problem-solving
Self-worth Revealer

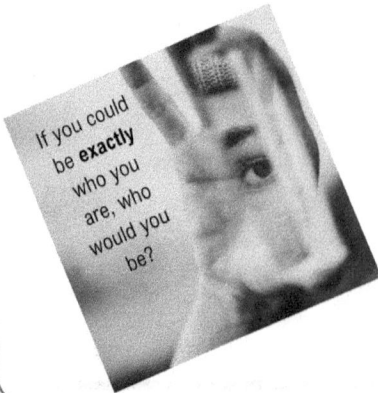

If you could be **exactly** who you are, who would you be?

The Medicine Drum can be used to heal yourself and others with the offering of love and gratitude through play, ceremonies and meditative journeying.

RECOMMENDED READING

Here is a list of books that have changed my life.

BOOK TITLE	AUTHOR
METAPHYSICAL ANATOMY Your Body is Talking, Are You Listening? Volume 1	Evette Rose
THE SECRET LANGUAGE OF YOUR BODY The Essential Guide to Health & Wellness	Inna Segal
THE MINDBODY PRESCRIPTION Healing the Body, Healing the Pain	John E. Sarno, M.D.
YOU CAN HEAL YOUR LIFE	Louise Hay
HOW TO GROW YOUR BUSINESS FASTER THAN YOUR COMPETITOR The Secrets to Freedom & Success in 5 Easy Steps	Sharon Jurd
VOICES OF IMPACT Empowering Stories from Female Visionaries and Entrepreneurs Volume 2	Compilation
THE SEVEN SPIRITUAL LAWS OF SUCCESS A Pocketbook Guide to Fulfilling Your Dreams	Deepak Chopra
THE ONE THING The Surprisingly Simple Truth Behind Extraordinary Results	Gary Keller with Jay Papasan
ATOMIC HABITS Tiny Changes, Remarkable Results	James Clear
BREAKING THE HABIT OF BEING YOURSELF How to Love Your Mind and Create a New One	Dr. Joe Dispenza
THE UNTETHERED SOUL The Journey Beyond Yourself	Michael A. Singer
THE BIOLOGY OF BELIEF Unleashing the Power of Consciousness, Matter & Miracles	Bruce H. Lipton, PH.D.
THE ASTONISHING POWER OF EMOTIONS Let Your Feelings Be Your Guide	Esther and Jerry Hicks
THE POWER OF INTENTION Learning to Co-create Your World Your Way	Dr. Wayne W. Dyer
SPIRITUAL PARTNERSHIP The Journey to Authentic Power	Gary Zukav
A NEW EARTH Awakening to Your Life's Purpose	Eckart Tolle

EVERYTHING IS HERE TO HELP YOU Finding the Gift in Life's Greatest Challenges	Matt Kahn
THE UNIVERSE ALWAYS HAS A PLAN The 10 Golden Rules of Letting Go	Matt Kahn
DARING GREATLY How the Courage to be Vulnerable Transforms the Way We Live, Love, Parent and Lead	Brené Brown PhD, LMSW
RISING STRONG How the Ability to Reset Transforms the Way We Live, Love, Parent and Lead	Brené Brown PhD, LMSW
DARE TO LEAD Brave Work, Tough Conversations, Whole Hearts	Brené Brown PhD, LMSW
OVERWORKED & UNDERLAID A Seriously Funny Guide to Life	Nigel Marsh
TOO SOON OLD, TOO LATE SMART Thirty True Things You Need to Know Now	Gordon Livingston M.D.
THE ONE MINUTE MANAGER	Ken Blanchard and Spencer Johnson
WHO MOVED MY CHEESE? An Amazing Way to Deal with Change in Your Work and in Your Life	Spencer Johnson M.D.
THE TOP FIVE REGRETS OF THE DYING A Life Transformed by the Dearly Departing	Bronnie Ware
THE HAPPIEST MAN ON EARTH A Holocaust Survivor Shares How He Found Gratitude, Kindness and Hope in the Darkest of Places	Eddie Jaku
THE BODY KEEPS THE SCORE Mind, Brain & Body in the Transformation of Trauma	Bessel Van der Kolk
BUILT TO MOVE The 10 Essential Habits to Help You Move Freely & Live Fully	Kelly Starrett & Juliet Starrett

www.ingramcontent.com/pod-product-compliance
Lightning Source LLC
Chambersburg PA
CBHW072153090426
42740CB00012B/2255